AF322616

This book is a must read for everyone who wants to make thoughtful, authentic decisions about their career and life path. You're not like a tree—you don't have to stay in the same place all the time. But having the courage to make a bold move is only part of the story. As Dr. McDaniel explains so well, there are many other factors to consider: Are you truly prepared? Do you have the necessary level of experience for success? Is that next step—be it a city or a job—the right fit? This book guides you through the kinds of thoughtful questions you've got to work through before making a major move, so you can make it with confidence.

What makes this book so valuable is how it encourages readers to look at themselves honestly—to examine their authenticity and assess whether an opportunity is genuinely appropriate for their goals. Fit is everything, and this book helps you understand if you're a fit for a certain position or path. Whether you are contemplating a bold move of your own or feeling as stuck as a tree rooted in place, this book can help you figure out the right path forward for *you*. Preparedness and authenticity—these are the keys to making decisions that will help you get more win-wins out of life.

—**Gene DeFilippo**, President, DeFilippo and Associates, LLC; Former Director of Athletics, Villanova University and Boston College

Whether you lead soldiers, employees, or fellow athletes, *Win-Win Leadership* is mandatory developmental reading. Dr. Karen McDaniel nails the critical gaps between leaders and those they lead on and off your field of competition in today's world.

—**Lieutenant Colonel Joseph Loar**, Retired Former Battalion Commander, 1-327 IN, 101st Airborne Division

Win-Win Leadership speaks directly to the quiet crisis unfolding in today's workplaces: People are starving for authenticity while leaders are burning out under models that no longer serve anyone. With clarity and compassion, Dr. McDaniel reframes authenticity not as oversharing or sentimentality, but as the disciplined alignment between values, self-awareness, and the courage to make bold, sometimes uncomfortable choices. What makes this book especially powerful is its insistence that growth does not require sacrifice or settling; true leadership creates conditions where individuals and organizations can thrive together. This is an essential guide for anyone ready to stop playing by outdated rules and start leading from a place of integrity, courage, and genuine collaboration.

—**Magdalena Fosse**, PsyD, PhD

Dr. Karen McDaniel has a gift for helping people see the leader within themselves. In *Win-Win Leadership*, she brings that same gift to every page, sharing her wisdom, courage, and authenticity in a way that makes you feel personally seen and inspired. Her message reminds us that true leadership isn't about titles or power; it's about purpose, empathy, and the courage to grow while lifting others.

—**Atin Suri**, CEO, Suri Hospitality Group

The author masterfully weaves captivating stories that immerse you in vivid landscapes of emotion and experience. I love her quote about "making decisions from a place of wisdom rather than a place of fear." I highly recommend it for anyone seeking a truly interesting read with stories that give you advice on making your life better.

—**Jim Corter**, President, Corter Consulting;
Strategic Leadership Coach

Win-Win Leadership is an insightful and great guide offering real strategies for leadership development. It is a must read for anyone looking to make a positive impact and grow as a leader!

—**Mark Young**, CEO and President,
Jonesboro Regional Chamber of Commerce

Karen McDaniel provides a concise, yet complete, guide to navigating around roadblocks to a leader's effectiveness and gaining critical interpersonal skills that can be leveraged to improve your leadership style.

—**Lexanne Horton**, Chief Financial Officer,
Ritter Communications

Dr. McDaniel's *Win-Win Leadership* redefines what it means to lead with heart and integrity. Her approach invites professionals to discover their authentic selves, navigate change with courage, and build genuine connections that drive lasting success. A must read.

—**Michael Stern**, CEO, Proventus;
Former US Naval Aviator

Win-Win Leadership is a must-read book on leadership that beautifully connects everyday life experiences to powerful leadership lessons. The "Bold" chapter especially stood out to me—it's inspiring, authentic, and truly empowering.

—**Rosey Flaherty**, CPA, MSA, Tax Manager,
BPM LLP; Forbes 2025 America's Top 200 CPAs

WIN-WIN
LEADERSHIP

WIN-WIN LEADERSHIP

KAREN R. McDANIEL, PhD

Unlocking Growth Through
Authenticity and **Collaboration**

Forbes | Books

Published by Forbes Books, Charleston, South Carolina.
An imprint of Advantage Media Group.

Forbes Books is a registered trademark, and the Forbes Books colophon is a trademark of Forbes Media, LLC.

Printed in the United States of America.

10 9 8 7 6 5 4 3 2 1

ISBN: 979-8-88750-777-4 (Hardcover)
ISBN: 979-8-88750-778-1 (eBook)
ISBN: 979-8-88750-779-8 (Audiobook)

Library of Congress Control Number: 2026900876

Cover design by Ruthie Wood.
Layout design by Lance Buckley.

This custom publication is intended to provide accurate information and the opinions of the author in regard to the subject matter covered. It is sold with the understanding that the publisher, Forbes Books, is not engaged in rendering legal, financial, or professional services of any kind. If legal advice or other expert assistance is required, the reader is advised to seek the services of a competent professional.

Since 1917, Forbes has remained steadfast in its mission to serve as the defining voice of entrepreneurial capitalism. Forbes Books, launched in 2016 through a partnership with Advantage Media, furthers that aim by helping business and thought leaders bring their stories, passion, and knowledge to the forefront in custom books. Opinions expressed by Forbes Books authors are their own. To be considered for publication, please visit **books.Forbes.com**.

02-10-2026 12:55

Those who teach us the most are often the hardest to quote. Therefore, this book is dedicated to my mother, Mayron Rogers, my biggest supporter and teacher. Growing up, she put everything she had into me and my future. Mom, you taught me to follow my dreams, to never give up, and to be strong. Thank you for always believing in me. I love you!

CONTENTS

INTRODUCTION 1

PHASE 1 17

Foundation
Understanding and Preparing Yourself

CHAPTER 1 19

Discovering Your Authentic Self

CHAPTER 2 33

Recognizing Your Worth

CHAPTER 3 47

Developing Mental Resilience

CHAPTER 4 59

Put Your Oxygen Mask on First

PHASE 2 71

Connection
Building Effective Relationships

CHAPTER 5 73

The Art of Effective Communication

CHAPTER 6 87

Mastering Conflict Resolution

CHAPTER 7 103

Building Meaningful Relationships

PHASE 3 119

Activation
Taking Bold Steps

CHAPTER 8 121

From Dreams to Action

CHAPTER 9 137

The Courage to Make Bold Moves

CHAPTER 10 151

Embracing Change as Opportunity

PHASE 4 161

Leadership
Creating Win-Win Impacts

CHAPTER 11 163

Leading with Authenticity

CHAPTER 12 175

Timing and Transitions

CHAPTER 13 187

Creating Your Win-Wins

CONCLUSION 197

Winds of Change

ADDITIONAL RESOURCES 199

ACKNOWLEDGMENTS 201

ABOUT THE AUTHOR 203

Five faces looked to me expectantly, waiting for me to speak. I carefully wiped the chalk dust off my hands, smoothed my shirt, and stood a little taller, mustering all the authority available to me as a self-confident seven-year-old.

"Now, for today's lesson, we'll be covering fractions." I cleared my throat and scribbled on the chalkboard *1/2 + 1/2 = ?* before turning back to my captive audience. Their silence didn't deter me.

"Yes, Pinky Baby?" I called on the baby doll sitting in the front row of my makeshift classroom, even though she hadn't moved to raise her hand. She was the most lifelike of the group, which was otherwise peppered with a mix of dolls homemade by my grandmother, some Barbies, a lifelike doll, and a variety of stuffed animals, along with my cat. Pinky Baby was the smaller version of my Pinky Honey doll. She had a soft pink cloth body and a plastic head featuring blue eyes with short lashes and a pert cherry-colored mouth—which, in my mind, now uttered a single word: "One."

Pinky Baby had come to class prepared that day, apparently. "Yes, that's correct," I said and nodded, confirming her imagined response. Seconds later, I was turning back to the chalkboard, filling in the answer: *1/2 + 1/2 = 2/2 = 1.*

This was how I spent many afternoons after school while growing up as an only child in small-town Tennessee. My grandfather, an army careerist who had served in the Second World War, was with the area's National Guard at the time, and he'd brought home an old chalkboard from work that would have otherwise ended up in the trash. To him, it was a toy for his granddaughter to play with. To me, it was a tool to teach with. I'd taken up "teaching" after school at age five, when the lessons had centered on basics such as spelling and reading. As I'd grown, the lessons had grown with me, and now, at age seven, fractions were the topic of the day.

That chalkboard, set up in the basement of my parents' home, became my classroom. I'd put a small table in front of it, on which I'd carefully placed my teaching materials—books, chalk, papers—and lined up my "students"—my dolls and stuffed animals. After school, I'd come home and teach them what I had learned that day, sharing the wealth of knowledge that school had provided me.

Those afternoons were magic to me. The screech of chalk against the blackboard and the feel of dust on my hands did not mar the satisfaction I got when my students excelled. (I admit: Pinky Baby was the star student.) I knew at five years old that I wanted to be a teacher. I didn't realize it completely then, but I was tapping into a part of myself that would continue to shape and define my adult years, finding an authentic joy in educating and coaching others that would ultimately define my career—and who I would become as a person.

These days, I'm no longer teaching fractions to baby dolls and stuffed animals—I'm coaching executives, managers, and professionals of all kinds on how to lead authentically and sustainably, in a way that honors their needs while contributing to others. Traditional command-and-control approaches that once defined successful leadership are now crumbling under the weight of remote work, generational shifts, and an increasingly diverse workforce that demands transparency and genuine connection. Employees are leaving jobs not because of poor pay or benefits but because they feel disconnected from leaders who seem inauthentic or solely focused on bottom-line results. Meanwhile, leaders themselves are burning out, caught between outdated playbooks and the real human needs of their teams. To thrive in this new era, leaders must learn to lead from their authentic selves, creating environments where everyone can win. That is the end goal of this book: getting to the win-wins, both at work and in life at large.

Making Bold Moves

> *"You don't have to have it all figured out to move forward."*
> —Original source unknown

"When I was your age, I didn't know where my next carton of milk was going to come from!" This was my father's first reaction to the news that I was planning on quitting my teaching job to get a PhD. My father had grown up very poor on a farm in rural Tennessee. He had worked hard to make sure that *I* never had to worry about where *my* next carton of milk was going to come from. And he and my mother had instilled in me early on the importance of smart finances and independence. They were thrilled that I'd gotten a high school teaching job, which promised security and a reliable pension—and my decision to leave that behind terrified them. But I was terrified, too—terrified that if I did *not* take this opportunity, I'd regret it for the rest of my life.

It's difficult to define my career by a single path. I transitioned from accounting to teaching high school math to leadership development in colleges of business and, finally, to executive coaching and consulting. My evolving career was driven by a fierce desire to keep on learning, and I had devoted fifteen years of my life to getting my education, including attending summer school and winter terms on top of the normal spring and fall terms. Whatever I was studying, I always saw it as a way of preparing for my next role, whatever that was.

The professional roles I've held have varied significantly, each coming with its own rewards and challenges, but they all share one thing: They involved helping others, not only imparting knowledge to them but also helping them to better understand their selves—how they best learn, communicate, and interact within ecosystems of other people, be it in a classroom or a boardroom. While it's easy to identify that red thread now, it wasn't always obvious to me amid the twists and turns of my winding career path.

Many of those twists and turns have been driven by bold moves that some might characterize as risky and others might characterize as foolish. You might also call them courageous. If you've ever considered a bold move yourself—quitting the job you hate but that pays well, taking the job you want but don't feel quite ready for, switching career tracks entirely—you know the stomach-churning feeling these decisions can create. They can also create wonderful opportunities.

The beginnings of my professional life were straightforward enough: I had a talent for numbers in middle and high school, so when I graduated, I went to community college to complete the training needed to become an accountant. But deep down, I knew that introverted job was not for me. I wanted to be out in the world, interacting with others, not sitting at a desk and crunching numbers, as I had an innate ability to understand people and interpersonal dynamics that I felt should be put to use. So, I went on to get a bachelor of science in business administration. It brought together my natural affinity for numbers and my desire to work with people, with its courses spanning management, mathematics, data processing, accounting, and secondary education.

When I graduated, I got a job as a math teacher at the local high school in my hometown of Lexington, Tennessee. I was living my childhood dream, standing in front of a chalkboard (although the math was a bit more complicated than the fractions I had taught Pinky Baby). Hungry for more, I also taught algebra two nights a week at the local community college and, for two years, spent one night a week pursuing my MBA.

It was toward the end of my MBA program that one of my professors approached me and said, "Karen, have you ever thought about getting your PhD?"

My initial response: "I'm just a small-town girl from West Tennessee! Me?"

Maybe I had not yet learned to recognize my own worth—but this professor saw something in me and shed a light on it that I could not at the time. With the idea planted in my mind, I started doing my research—and the more I learned about the possibility, the more interested I got. I decided to go for it. It was a bold decision, leaving behind the security of my teaching job—especially given that I'd just received my MBA, which meant an automatic pay raise—but it felt right, and I greeted the change of plans, scary as it was, with enthusiasm.

While my mother, my eternal cheerleader, shared my enthusiasm, my father was more hesitant. He asked a lot of questions: "Aren't you worried about losing your benefits? What about retirement planning?" He was baffled by my decision to throw away a career path that promised security to step into the unknown world of academia.

In an effort to make me rethink my decision, my father trotted out his milk carton line. I reassured my parents that I had a plan in place and had done the math to make sure I'd be able to cover my milk cartons (as well as other necessities, such as student insurance) while studying. I did mention that a PhD was essentially a guarantee of a very high-paying job, although it would be a lot of work and might take many years to get tenure.

Still, despite my own nebulous future and my parents' well-intentioned concerns, I went ahead and got my PhD in organizational behavior, human resource management, and strategic management, with additional studies in neuropsychology and marketing. Eventually, my parents came around. And I never looked back. It was a bold move that would ultimately pay off.

Teaching Leadership, Learning Myself

"Stop shrinking yourself to fit places you've outgrown."
—Original source unknown

Before I even got my PhD, I had long recognized that I preferred teaching adults rather than children. I thrived in the classroom when I was able to exchange ideas with my students, providing direction and guidance while also being challenged by others' ideas. Maybe part of that came from being an only child who grew up in a rural area. I never spent much time around young kids—I was more often surrounded by adults: my parents and grandparents, people at church, and so forth. The adult world of academia thus suited me very well—but it wasn't until I started teaching courses in leadership development that I really hit my stride.

When I began teaching at universities in Tennessee, Virginia, and Arkansas, I was given courses covering a range of topics, from organizational behavior to human resource (HR) management. Later, I moved on to graduate-level organizational behavior and leadership development. Throughout this experience, I didn't enjoy the HR side of things as much, as HR is more policy driven. I was far more interested in the behavioral side and how people interact and get along—motivation, perception, personality, conflict resolution, and emotional intelligence.

Then I started teaching at the graduate level—and that's when it really clicked: *This is fabulous!* I was teaching adults from all walks of life: aspiring CEOs, military veterans, and international students from Kuwait, Nepal, Saudi Arabia, China, Japan, India, France, and beyond. And I had the opportunity to help them not only learn but also level up their careers. Teaching a subject such as math, English, or history is very different from teaching people how to lead: how to recognize their own strengths and weaknesses, develop their unique leadership style, and communicate with others effectively, regardless of position, personality type, or professional title.

I was adamant about one thing: I wanted my students to actually *learn* leadership, not just read about it. I wanted to go beyond a prescriptive syllabus, coursework, and exams. So, I created a leadership development class for the graduate program—and I invited my students to help me.

On the first day of the course, I put the desks in a circle, arranging my students as carefully as I had once arranged my dolls in my parents' basement, and put my own chair in the middle. As my students entered the room, they looked at me, puzzled, wondering about the unusual classroom setup.

I told them, "I'm going to sit here in the middle of the group—and I would like for you all to help me write the syllabus for this new course. I'm going to give you a few parameters, but I want your help fulfilling my vision for this class."

And so they did. From day one, they had buy-in because they'd helped create the course criteria, and I discovered that allowing them to set the standards empowered them while also holding them accountable.

That class became one of the most interesting and challenging I ever taught. Instead of using a textbook, I gave my students articles to read—a lot of them from *Harvard Business Review*, whose pieces are more hands-on and applicable than just theoretical academic papers. The students could read the articles on their own time; I just asked that they kept journal entries about their reading as a graded assignment.

Throughout the course, we also referred to the DISC behavioral profile and manual, which will be described further in chapter 5. DISC is a behavioral assessment tool that categorizes people into four main personality or communication styles. I am certified by TTI Success Insights to administer and interpret DISC behavioral assessments, helping individuals and teams improve their communication, performance, and self-awareness. The acronym DISC stands for dominance, influence, steadiness, and conscientiousness: the four key behavior traits that all individuals embody. It's important to note that *every* person embodies *all* these traits, just to varying degrees.

I asked my students to incorporate DISC into their interactions with others—and I made sure that they had opportunities for a *lot* of interactions. There weren't any tests in this class. Instead, we went out into the community for real-world learning. For example, we raised money for St. Jude's Children's Research Hospital—and then we visited the hospital, where the CFO (an alumnus of the university) gave us a tour and spoke about professional development. Here, we heard the difficult stories about what had brought the kids to the hospital and learned where the money we'd raised had gone, including the sorts of research it had funded. Additionally, my students put together hundreds of craft kits for patients.

I also required my students to attend chamber of commerce events, such as receptions and seminars. They would come dressed professionally and with their business cards in hand, ready to hand out if they connected with someone. I also asked them to have their résumés updated and ready to send out at a moment's notice—just in case they met someone on-site who said, "Hey, I have a job opening." Preparation made the promise of possibility more tangible. And when the students gave their final presentation at the end of the semester, I encouraged them to invite any contacts they had made, telling them, "You never know what might come of it."

This business leadership course fulfilled a vision I'd been creating in my mind for a long time. I was trying to build something where students got out into the community and actually learned the practice of business leadership—rather than just sitting in a classroom, reading a book, and taking a test. In doing so, in encouraging them to forge connections and build relationships, I wanted them to see how leadership could be used in service of others.

Service has been central to my career in many ways. I have done many leadership programs and initiatives at local, state, regional, and national levels. One initiative I'm especially proud of is my appointment to the Delta Leadership Institute Executive Academy by the governor of Arkansas. This initiative brings together people from eight states in the Delta region—all economically challenged rural areas—to work on issues such as broadband access, clean water, and sustainable resources. Such acts of service have always been fulfilling to me as well as professionally productive, helping me make valuable connections. When I first moved to various states, I didn't know a soul, and my community service was critical to building my network. I wanted my students to recognize the benefit of such relationship building early on in their careers.

In helping my students go beyond the classroom and step into the real world, I encouraged them to take steps to identify their authentic selves—to consider their gifts, question their purpose, and understand where they could contribute to society. It was immensely gratifying to see many of them come into their own and gain confidence—the same kind of confidence I'd called on when I'd decided to make the bold move to leave the security of my teaching job and pursue a PhD.

But while I watched my students make their bold moves and head forth into the world, something kept coming up in my mind. Was *I* in the right place? For the most part, I felt I was doing exactly what I was supposed to be doing—and excelling at it. I had won numerous teaching and service awards. I had served as department chair, graduate program director, and faculty athletics representative (FAR), which led to the regional and national roles of Sun Belt Conference FAR chair and NCAA FARA executive committee member. I had achieved everything a faculty member could achieve, but I didn't aspire to become a dean or chancellor—the logical next step—as such a role would encase me in the executive world, away from the students I loved to work with.

The question then became, *What's next?* It would take an unexpected offer—and another bold move—to figure out the answer.

Finding the Courage to Step into Authenticity

"Don't be afraid to start over. It's a chance to build something better this time." —Original source unknown

My exit from academia was unexpected. It began when I was appointed by a provost to be on a dean search committee responsible for choosing an executive search firm. We reviewed five firms, interviewed three over Zoom, and selected one to come to campus. When the executive from the search firm arrived, I introduced myself, mentioning that we'd met on the Zoom call.

Five minutes into the conversation, he looked at me and said, in front of the entire dean search committee, "I'm going to hire you!" The he paused, catching what he'd said, and added, "When you're finished with higher education." I literally looked down at my watch to check the time—marking the moment when my future shifted.

In the back of my mind, I had always thought I might want to work in leadership consulting and executive coaching. But this aspiration was always intended for "someday"—after retirement, maybe fifteen or twenty years down the road. I hadn't planned to leave academia until then. Then came that pivotal conversation with the executive search consultant, and something clicked. I had aligned my work as best as possible with the things I was most passionate about—for example, my leadership development course, which focused so heavily on engaged teaching and active service. Still, I wondered, could I be doing more?

Soon thereafter, I was talking with that executive search firm's senior global VP, the CFO, and the rest of the team. The firm had a department that specialized in academic searches for deans, presidents, and chancellors. I realized this was an unprecedented opportunity to make a significant career change. If I didn't take it, I might be stuck in academia forever. I believe in setting deliberate goals, so I took a piece of paper, wrote *Leave academia* at the top, and then listed the things I needed to do to make that happen—get a new business suit, find a financial advisor, secure strong references, and a few other key steps. Most importantly, I put a date on it: July 2022. It was already March, which gave me only a small window of time. But I did it. My last day in academia was July 31, 2022.

After that amazing corporate experience, I decided to devote myself fully to my leadership consulting, speaking, and executive coaching business, Empowering Executives, which I started in 2011 as a side venture alongside my academic career. The company offers tailored solutions to help leaders unlock their full potential through consulting and speaking engagements. Throughout my career, I have worked with people from all walks of life and from all over the world: hoteliers, athletes, C-suite executives, and even pageant queens. And in this new role—a far cry from teaching high school math, where my journey began—I have come into my own. I feel more like myself than I did in the twenty-plus years I spent in academia.

When I left academia, I expected people to be shocked. I'd had a great job with excellent security, and I'd excelled at it. *Why leave?*

However, I was pleasantly surprised by the reality of the situation. One of my former supervisors called me after I shared my news. He said, "I just want to tell you how much I admire your courage." He explained that he'd had opportunities to leave the university many times but had always found it too hard to walk away from the security. "I couldn't do it," he admitted.

Several others in academia expressed similar sentiments—they'd wanted to leave or had even received offers to leave, but the bold move had eluded them. When I broke the news to my family, I half expected my father to tell me his milk carton story, but things had changed since the days when I'd quit teaching to pursue a PhD. I had changed. He simply said, "I'm not surprised." Maybe my father saw, before I did, that my job in academia was not the end of the line, career-wise, for me. He told me I had been blessed with a special gift.

Since starting Empowering Executives, I've learned that being bold and courageous sounds fun and exciting—but it can also be frightening. Many of the people I've worked with over the years have expressed feelings of fear, anxiety, and sometimes, loneliness. Helping them tune into their natural selves and gain the conviction needed to make sound decisions that allow for bold moves has been fabulous. And that is what I hope to do for you, with this book.

In the pages that follow, we'll discuss what it takes to get to the win-wins, creating outcomes that benefit both you and those around you through authentic leadership. The book is broken into four phases:

- ✿ **Foundation**—Understanding and Preparing Yourself, which helps you discover your authentic self, recognize your worth, develop mental resilience and tenacity, and learn to put your own oxygen mask on first

- ✿ **Connection**—Building Effective Relationships, which covers the art of effective communication and building meaningful relationships

- ✿ **Activation**—Taking Bold Steps, which guides you from dreams to action, helps you find the courage to make bold moves, and teaches you to embrace change as opportunity

- ✿ **Leadership**—Creating Win-Win Impacts, which shows you how to lead authentically and create outcomes where everyone benefits

Each chapter will share broader theoretical ideas and conclude with an exercise you can use to engage with those ideas, spurring you on your authenticity journey. Because I want this book to be practical, not just theoretical—something that you walk away from feeling changed by. Think of these exercises as pearls of wisdom—each one a gem of insight that you can gather, hold, and apply to your own life.

But the pearls don't stop there. You'll also see that I've included quotes throughout the book, under the chapter headers. There's a history to these quotes, which I've compiled over many years. It started when I was teaching my graduate-level business leadership development classes in an MBA program. Although we only discussed professional topics in class, I'd notice when students were struggling, be it for academic or personal reasons. So when I had a quote that seemed to fit their situation, I'd send it to them—a small acknowledgment of their struggle and encouragement to carry on. Over time, I extended this practice to colleagues, professional acquaintances, and people who attended my presentations. We can all use this kind of encouragement at times, so I've included some of my favorite such quotes throughout the book to support you as you embark on this authenticity journey. These quotes are pearls too—small, luminous truths that can light your way when the path seems unclear.

This journey is one that is both professional and personal because the lessons that apply to your career—things such as how to communicate—will also apply to your personal life. While I envision this book being for leaders or aspiring leaders, particularly those ready to take that next step up the ladder, it can extend beyond that sphere as well. Many of these concepts work for both professional and personal development—sometimes, they overlap significantly. By the time you reach the final page, you'll have gathered a full necklace of pearls of wisdom—practical exercises and inspiring words strung together to support your journey toward living authentically.

Whether you're a newly minted CEO, working your way up the career ladder, or simply seeking clarity as to where you're headed personally or professionally, my hope is that you can capture the magic of unlocking your authentic self not only in work but in life—that you can walk away empowered, confident, motivated, and optimistic. Ready to conquer whatever lies ahead of you. Ready to get to the win-wins.

Foundation

*Understanding and
Preparing Yourself*

Discovering Your Authentic Self

I have a cow to thank for one of my early job offers in academia—at least, that's how I remember it. A cow—and my dad. My parents taught me how to work hard. They were employed at a bank and ran the family's small farm. Basically, they had two jobs. They would get home at a quarter past five on the dot, eat a quick dinner, and then be out working the farm until dark. The farm had horses and cows—and cats. I was only two years old when my dad got me my first kitten of my own—I was elated and have had at least one cat ever since.

When I was a little girl, I wanted to be just like my dad. He rode horses, so I wanted to ride horses too. He was out in the fields with the cows; my parents got me a toy farm truck with cows. There was one type of cow in particular that captivated my imagination as a young girl: the Oreo cow. If you're familiar with the snack—with its sugar-laden white filling pressed between two black cookies—you can imagine what an "Oreo cow" looked like. This type of dairy cow, more accurately known as a Holstein Friesian, is notable for its distinctive black and white markings. Though this phase of my childhood didn't last long, as shopping with my mom soon became more fun, I learned good lessons on the farm.

When I was applying to academic jobs early in my career, one of the higher education institutions I interviewed with was an agricultural school. During my interview visit, the department chair drove me around the farm that belonged to the school—and lo and behold, there was a herd of Oreo cows. I was delighted and shared that I'd grown up on a farm with my own Oreo cow. That small kernel of truth sparked a lively conversation about farm life that helped me form an authentic connection with the department chair. I believe that conversation played a small part in my landing the job—largely because I had allowed my authentic self to shine through.

The term *authenticity* gets thrown around a lot these days, and everyone has their own interpretation of the word—you could probably ask fifty different people and get fifty different definitions—so it's helpful to elucidate what I mean by it in this context. To me, authenticity is simply being true to yourself and your needs, wants, and wishes. Some people mistakenly conflate authenticity with transparency, assuming that sharing everything about themselves demonstrates genuineness. But authenticity isn't about disclosure; it's about self-awareness and alignment between your inner truth and your actions. It's about understanding and honoring your core values, desires, and motivations without feeling compelled to broadcast every detail to the world.

You can be completely authentic while still maintaining appropriate boundaries about what you choose to share with others. The key is ensuring that what you do share and how you present yourself genuinely reflect who you are rather than whom you think others want you to be. The question then becomes, *Who are you* really?

Peeling Back the Layers to Discover Authenticity

> *"Sometimes when you are in the dark place[,] you think you have been buried, but you've actually been planted."* –Attributed to Christine Caine[1]

As an educator and a coach, I have worked with people from all walks of life. I've trained future business leaders in higher ed classrooms. I've coached Miss Arkansas and Miss Tennessee candidates (two of whom won Miss Arkansas and went on to compete in Miss America). Several times, I helped the individuals of a university baseball team, along with numerous other athletes in a variety of sports, identify their distinct behavior profiles using DISC assessments. Across the board, whether I was working with a pageant competition winner, an athlete, or a future CEO, I witnessed one thing again and again: The people I worked with blossomed once they were able to step into their own authentic selves—in many cases, doing so helped them define a clear purpose.

I had one all-star class in the leadership development course I taught that really drove this fact home for me. All the students I taught over the years were fabulous. But this group—one of the last cohorts I would teach—really shone. It was a very international group, which may have been part of the magic. When I was an educator, I always said that I learned more from my international students than they did from me, and this group exemplified that. The countries represented included China, India, France, and Kuwait. The students ranged from about age twenty to mid-forty and came from diverse backgrounds.

---

1   Christine Caine (@ChristineCaine), "Sometimes when you're in a dark place you think you've been buried, but you've actually been planted," X, August 13, 2023, https://x.com/ChristineCaine/status/1690752319275905024.

One student was current military, for example, while another came from the hospitality industry.

As I'd done in previous semesters, I got the students heavily involved in service projects, both individual and group endeavors. I asked them to attend business events. And I presented them with a new challenge: Help me take the course online. The school's MBA program was preparing to launch the course as a distance-learning option, and I wanted to test the waters before it started. The timing was fortuitous; it was early 2020, and a couple of months into the semester, the world would shut down because of the COVID-19 pandemic. Since we'd already started preparing for the switch, this class was able to complete the remainder of the course online—even the five-course dining etiquette portion, which I'd usually have done in a restaurant. Instead, we did it on Zoom, with my students gamely sitting at their desks rather than a table with a white table-cloth. They pushed through that tumultuous time and helped me put the entire class online for future semesters. Then they went on to pursue their various professional paths—and they really shone, each one in their own way.

The young man from Kuwait—who you will hear from in chapter 7—went on to build his own hotel from the ground up and became deeply involved in the local community. When I later became chair of the local chamber of commerce board, he was one of the two people I appointed to the board. I wanted the board to have greater diversity to represent the younger professionals, and I knew that he would bring a fresh and worldly perspective. He didn't disappoint, as his unique background and entrepreneurial spirit made a valuable addition, providing to the board many different ideas about what the city needed to thrive.

Another student from that class is now part of that chamber's young professionals network. I've watched her flourish as she balances working for a financial firm with building her own marketing business, and I remain inspired by her. We still meet for lunch periodically. She recently had a baby but continues to pursue her entrepreneurial dreams relentlessly, balancing motherhood and business life with a grace and poise I admire.

Then there is Ana, who exemplifies resilience—or what she likes to call "stubbornness"—in ways I could never have imagined. Ana was in my first leadership development class, the one that helped me build the syllabus. She was battling breast cancer during her MBA and was unable to attend her graduation because of her treatments. We organized a special surprise ceremony for her, with her family present, because her dedication to the program despite such personal challenges embodied everything that leadership class was meant to teach. Since then, Ana and her husband have started a business that has become quite successful in the community. They are now active chamber members who sponsor events—and Ana was recently awarded a "Women to Watch" award by a local city magazine.

UNLOCKING AUTHENTICITY

Ana Saucedo, Director of Marketing and Finance, Swept Away Janitorial

Some people have used the word resilient to describe me, but I honestly think of myself as stubborn—and I mean that in a good way. When I set my mind to do something, I want to finish it. After my breast cancer diagnosis, I was determined to finish my MBA. It felt like not finishing was not an option.

Dr. McDaniel and the other professors at the university were incredibly supportive throughout this time, and when they organized a surprise mini graduation ceremony for me, that was the moment when I realized, I did it. It was a heartfelt moment—my coworkers, professors, classmates, and family were all there, and they had really thought of every detail. They'd even picked up my cap and gown so I could put them on and walk.

After graduating, my husband and I cofounded Swept Away, a janitorial and commercial cleaning company that now serves five school districts in Arkansas. I apply everything I learned from my MBA to handle the back-end administration. But what really sets our company apart from the competition isn't our service; it's our genuine community involvement—something I learned from Dr. McDaniel.

I come from a working family in Mexico, and the idea of networking to build authentic relationships is something we never discussed. Now that I'm managing a business, I see firsthand how authentic connection benefits us and those around us. By giving back time, money, and energy to our community, we have built a strong network of support and been able to thrive as a business.

I think the thing that is most important to me is the sense of authentic purpose this gives me. I don't want to be defined by any single label or experience. I don't want to be labeled as "Ana the survivor" or "Ana the businesswoman." The truth·is, you are not defined by the things that happened to you but by what you do with those situations. In an odd way, my cancer experience forced me to discover what truly mattered to me and how to live more authentically—which is exactly what Dr. McDaniel helped us uncover.

Ana's story speaks to the success that can come with a bit of tenacity—what she might call "stubbornness." The trajectories of the various young women I coached for Miss Arkansas have proven similarly inspiring. One of these women went on to become a news anchor in Kentucky. Another became a physician's liaison at one of the biggest hospitals in Arkansas. And another is now a pharmacist. They've all gone on to be successful in their own ways.

At first glance, these individuals appear to be very different from one another. Different countries of origin, cultures, aspirations, and personal experiences. But they all share something: an unwavering commitment to authenticity. They were all willing to do the work, peel back the layers of the onion, and answer those tough questions: *Who am I? What do I stand for? What do I believe in? What do I wish for?* And as you define your own path and purpose, you'll want to do the same.

Authenticity requires courage because, in the process of unveiling yourself and figuring out your purpose, you'll often be forced to question existing assumptions you have about yourself or to make decisions that lead to bold moves. That can be scary. But the opposite—staying in a place, position, or state of mind that doesn't align with your values, desires, and motivations—is even scarier, as well as miserable.

Authenticity also requires integrity. Integrity is another one of those words that probably has a million different definitions depending on whom you ask. To me, it means staying wholly true to your principles without compromise. That can get difficult in the search for authenticity because you may encounter people who do not *want* you to peel back the layers and discover their purpose.

A Win-Win Exercise
Unlock the Power of Your Authentic Self

Authenticity often reveals itself most clearly when we're in our element—those moments when time seems to fly by and we feel completely absorbed in what we're doing. This exercise will help you identify patterns in your life that point toward your authentic self.

Part 1: Reflection Questions

Take a few minutes to think about and write down your responses to these questions:

1. Passion points: What are three things you're genuinely passionate about? These can be personal, professional, or a mix of both.

2. Flow moments: Describe three times in your life when you felt completely in the zone—when you lost track of time because you were so engaged in what you were doing. What were you doing? What made these experiences so compelling?

3. Courageous dreams: What are three bold moves or changes you'd like to make over the next three years? Don't worry about how realistic they seem right now—just focus on what genuinely excites or calls to you.

Part 2: Pattern Recognition

Look at your answers above and consider the following:

1. What themes or patterns do you notice across your responses?
2. What activities or environments seem to bring out your best self?
3. What values or motivations appear repeatedly in your answers?

Part 3: Your Authentic Self Statement

Based on your reflections, complete this sentence: "I feel most like my authentic self when I am ..." Keep your responses somewhere you can revisit them as you continue through this book. These insights will guide you as you explore how to align your leadership style with who you truly are.

Remember: There are no right or wrong answers here. The goal is simply to begin peeling back the layers and getting curious about what makes you uniquely you.

I've always advised people I've taught or coached to be true to who they are. When they're faced with difficult decisions or challenging questions, I encourage them to answer honestly and from their heart—to express not what they think they're supposed to say or do or what they think someone thinks they are supposed to say or do, but what genuinely reflects who they are and how they want to show up in the world.

As you prepare to peel back the layers, accept that there may be setbacks and that it might get scary. But know that it's all so very worth it. Because while you might face moments of darkness, they are only temporary—and once out of those moments of reckoning, you're destined to bloom.

Moving Beyond Your Comfort Zone to Find Purpose

> *"Where you are a year from now is a reflection of the choices you choose to make right now."* –Original source unknown

Whatever your reference point—whether you grew up in the United States or elsewhere, whether you're from a big city or a rural farm, whether you work in a big company or are an entrepreneur—you can benefit from getting in touch with your true self. With that said, discovering your authentic self is not an overnight process. It takes time and often happens in infinitesimal steps. Even if you think you've already tapped into your authentic self, sometimes you peel back one more layer and find that there is still more to discover.

Take my own case. While I was in academia, I was convinced that I was doing exactly what I was supposed to be doing. It didn't feel wrong or off; I wasn't unhappy. I was striving and thriving, advancing up the career ladder and enjoying myself along the way. But it wasn't 100 percent right for me.

To get tenure in academia, you're generally evaluated on three components: research, service, and teaching. Research is generally considered the most important. However, while I actively participated in all three of these components as an academic, my priorities were the inverse: I loved the teaching and service elements but was less enthusiastic about the research. It was only after I stepped out of academia that I was able to fully lean into the teaching and service components that aligned with my authentic self. But this required leaving my comfort zone.

One of the best things you can do to get to the core of who you really are and identify your fundamental values, desires, and motivations is to get out of your comfort zone. When I was working as an educator, I was constantly seeking out new experiences for my students, trying to find ways to challenge them. One semester, we visited a hotel construction site. It was winter, freezing cold, and there was ice on the steel beams as we walked through the site, hard hats firmly on our heads.

Another semester, I had a student who was a biochemist in my graduate leadership class. He was a very intelligent man, and I remember asking him, "You have a PhD and run a lab of your own ... What are you doing here?" He candidly told me, "I know my science. I don't know people." He wanted help learning how to manage his team. After he'd completed my course, I asked him if I could bring the next semester's students to the lab for a visit—and he agreed! We put our white coats on, toured the lab, and extracted the DNA of strawberries.

As a coach, I'd similarly try to find ways to get the people I worked with out of their comfort zones, encouraging them to explore different contexts and forge new connections. I used to speak to chamber of commerce groups and leadership teams, and I would have each participant complete a bingo-style networking game. They'd be given a matrix of characteristics or experiences they had to find among the people in the room by asking them questions—for example, "Have you ever been to Europe?" So they had to go around the room, introduce themselves, shake hands, and then ask and discuss those questions. The aim was to try to build relationships.

That bingo card always included one question that may have seemed a little out of left field at first.

"Have you ever seen an Oreo cow in person?"

Now, I'd have them play this game. Afterward, I'd share my own Oreo cow story—a story that demonstrated how a random commonality (cows!) could connect two people. And part of the reason I'd include that question was because I wanted them to come and ask it of *me*, the speaker/coach. For some, approaching the person in charge can be extremely intimidating, and I wanted to give them a reason to strike up a conversation with me, the speaker, even if it was nerve-racking.

Those small steps beyond what we are used to, beyond what's easy, are what gives us the confidence to later make the bold moves that can change our lives. But you've got to practice. And that starts with getting out of your comfort zone—which admittedly requires some courage. I confess, it took some courage to quit my teaching job and get a PhD and, later, to leave academia to build and ultimately run my own business full-time. But with each courageous step, my world expanded, and I gave myself permission to dream bigger. You never know where the small steps you take today will land you in a year or two. The key is to take the first step, even if you can't see where the path will lead just yet.

What enabled these students to achieve such remarkable success? Beyond their diverse backgrounds and experiences, they all demonstrated two qualities essential to authentic leadership: courage and integrity.

Finding the Courage to Be Authentic with Integrity

"Some people will never like you because your spirit irritates their demons." —Attributed to Denzel Washington

I know a woman who's spent her entire career in the finance industry. She has good job security, but she doesn't really like what she's doing. She's thought about exploring other options but is afraid that if someone at her office finds out, she'll get fired. She already knows that her current role isn't authentically her. Yet fear holds her back from making a bold move.

Even once we've made the bold move, fear can be a factor. I've met new CEOs who are petrified, who feel like they don't know what they're doing but need to project confidence and competence nonetheless. When I congratulated one such individual on his new role, he smiled wryly and told me, "It feels like I'm trying to drink water from a fire hydrant."

There are people who may try to hold you back or bring you down as you commence this journey toward authenticity. Let them try (or, in the words of author and speaker Mel Robbins, simply, "Let them!"). And if those people try to ruffle your feathers? In the words of another bold woman, Taylor Swift, "Shake it off." Focus on yourself and your purpose. It will be well worth it.

Sometimes, even when we think we've found our purpose and achieved success, we discover there's another layer to peel back. David Brooks writes about this phenomenon in his book *The Second Mountain*, in which he describes how we can climb what we believe is our mountain of success—accomplishing goals, feeling successful, checking all the boxes—only to reach the summit and realize there's another mountain across the valley. That's when we understand that what we thought was our true calling may have just been preparation for our real purpose.

This realization can be both exhilarating and exhausting. I've seen this with professionals who've spent years building what they thought was their dream career, only to find themselves physically and emotionally drained—suffering from what many call adrenal fatigue. The stress of living misaligned with our authentic purpose takes a real toll on our bodies and minds, affecting everything from our cardio-vascular health to our cortisol levels. The woman I mentioned who's stuck in finance exemplifies this perfectly. Years ago, she probably thought finance offered security and success. She's done well and has job security, but she's not happy. If you're not happy, you're likely not living your purpose. As the saying goes, "If you're doing what you love, you'll never work a day in your life."

Too many people settle—for jobs, partners, cities, situations—all while secretly dreaming of something else. If you don't believe change is possible, you're right because with that mindset, you will be in the exact same place next year. To believe change *is* possible, you've got to know your worth—which we'll discuss in the next chapter.

CHAPTER 2

Recognizing Your Worth

Sometimes it takes someone else's perspective to help us fully recognize the value we already add—and the potential we have yet to unlock. Such was the case for Mariana, a talented musician who came to me wanting to shift career tracks. She had already achieved amazing things professionally, earning a BA in music and working as a musician in various contexts, including playing trombone for Adele's backing orchestra.

When Mariana and I first met, she was thinking of going back to school to get her bachelor's in management. I was department chair at the time and was holding meetings with international students who were interested in the business track.

It took only a brief conversation with her to convince me that she had the tenacity and drive needed for an MBA. So I said to her, "You already have an undergraduate degree. Instead of getting another one, why not try for an MBA?"

She was taken aback but pleasantly surprised by this turn of events. She'd walked into the room expecting to discuss her enrollment in a bachelor's program, only to be told she should aim higher. Understandably, her head was spinning. Nonetheless, she was perceptive enough to know that if the opportunity was there, she should grab it with both hands.

It must have taken quite a bit of courage for her to make the leap from music to an MBA program. However, she went for it, not only successfully completing the program while working as my graduate assistant for two years but also interning at a hotel. Once she had completed her MBA, she took a marketing job for a major hospitality group that owned the hotel she'd interned with, managing the marketing for upward of thirty properties. Later, she went on to work for an industry-leading commerce media technology company. I look forward to seeing where her path takes her—I have no doubt that it will continue to climb upward.

That kind of exponential growth requires knowing what you're worth. While Mariana was already driven and confident when our paths crossed, she didn't see herself as a future MBA. Much like I had never considered a PhD until a professor suggested it to me, she needed someone else to say, "Hey, you could do this. This is possible."

Such situations remind me of the adage that you need to know your worth and then add tax. As confident as someone may be, sometimes it still takes an extra nudge for them to fully appreciate their worth or, perhaps better said, to recognize their potential. In my case, a professor added the tax for me. In Mariana's case, I took on that role. While having these kinds of cheerleaders in life is fabulous, we should ideally be able to do the calculation of "full worth plus tax" on our own. Like Mariana, we often need someone else to point out our potential before we can see it ourselves. But how do we develop the ability to recognize our own worth?

The Key to Self-Worth: Building Confidence Without Arrogance

"If you have the power to eat alone in a restaurant or sit alone in a cinema hall, then you can do anything in your life."
—Original source unknown

When I was a young woman, my grandmother told me I didn't need a date to go out to dinner at a restaurant—I could go by myself and enjoy it. So, I did. She was teaching me a valuable lesson in self-worth and confidence.

Every person has challenges when it comes to recognizing their worth, regardless of their personality style. It's not necessarily insecurity that holds us back. It could be overanalyzing, perfectionism, stalling, acting too fast, or other patterns that cause you to hold back, hesitate to lean into your authenticity, or doubt yourself or your decisions.

Consider these challenges in terms of DISC behavioral styles; each style will face its own hurdles. While *S* (steadiness) and *C* (conscientiousness) personalities may struggle with indecision and overanalysis, *D* (dominance) styles may come across as too bold, and *I* (influence) styles may struggle with impulsiveness.

Each DISC style has its own strengths and weaknesses, and understanding your DISC style can help you identify the specific patterns around your self-worth and decision-making habits, allowing you to develop strategies that work *with* your natural tendencies rather than against them. In chapter 5, I'll dive deeper into the DISC behavioral styles, and while some of these may mean that someone presents as more confident, that doesn't mean that person doesn't wrestle with questions of self-worth—and those wrestling matches can take many forms, depending on the person.

Challenges with self-worth can also translate to imposter syndrome. I first learned this term from a young woman I was coaching who was worried she "had it," phrasing her concern as if imposter syndrome were a contagious disease. She was a high school teacher who was studying marketing and questioning whether she belonged in the marketing world—she was unsure if she deserved a seat at the table. I advised her to follow the advice of social psychologist and Harvard researcher Amy Cuddy, and "Fake it till you become it." That doesn't mean you need to fake it or lie to people. It's simply about telling yourself, "I can do this. One step at a time; I can do this." That coaching client went on to have an impressive marketing career working for a major agriculture company. Would that have been possible if she hadn't articulated and addressed her insecurities head-on? I'm not sure.

Everyone has some kind of insecurity, whether they acknowledge it aloud or not. While teaching, I witnessed many of my international students express uncertainty about their English skills. I would remind them, "You speak *two* languages. You have international experience. You have multicultural experience. I wish I could speak two languages." They were looking in the mirror and seeing deficiency; looking at that same reflection, I could see something quite different—strength.

How can we get a clear vision of ourselves in that metaphorical mirror—a vision that accurately reflects all our worth and potential so that we never hesitate to take the next step in life? It requires building self-confidence. However, confidence doesn't equal arrogance. Just as the mirror can lie to us if it doesn't show our full worth, it can also lie to us if it inflates what we are capable of.

When someone gets so self-confident that they become arrogant, thinking they are superior to others, there's usually a downfall coming. This is why it's important to stay humble and remember where you came from. Every part of your story, including where you started, has helped shape who you are. Or, as my dad used to put it, "Remember your roots, and never put on your cocky pants."

For Mariana, recognizing her value (plus tax) meant embracing her atypical past as a musician—and her international background, having been born in Costa Rica—and translating that to a new career in business. She has done so, with great success.

ELEVATING SELF-WORTH

Mariana Cisneros Serrano,

Senior Program Operations Coordinator, Koddi

Before I have a big meeting, I always do a power pose: hands on hips, feet shoulder-width apart, chest proud, and chin high! It might sound silly, but it definitely makes me feel more confident and releases any nervous energy I might have. The power pose is something I learned from Dr. McDaniel, and it's become a part of my regular routine, helping me show up as my best self.

When I first met Dr. McDaniel, I was a musician transitioning out of an intense professional period. I had been living in New York, working in music, and I loved it—but I needed a break. The career path of a musician didn't feel sustainable, so I decided to get an undergraduate degree in management. Then, I met Dr. McDaniel. She heard my story and advocated for me to pursue an MBA instead—something I hadn't even considered possible at that time.

Dr. McDaniel taught me a lot of practical skills that built my confidence, from how to be diplomatic to the power of silent language. She also taught me the mindset of, "We'll figure it out." She would always say that—regardless of what challenges came up, the answer was always that we could figure it out.

After graduation, I started working for a hotel, supervising their housekeeping department. It wasn't exactly the role I had dreamed of post-MBA, but it was during COVID-19, and companies weren't really hiring. I decided to make the most of my time there and connected with the property's digital marketing and e-commerce manager via LinkedIn, scheduling regular meetings to learn from her—and when she moved to another company, she recommended that I apply for her position. Even with her encouragement, I struggled with imposter syndrome. But I remembered Dr. McDaniel's advice: "Fake it until you become it—originated by Dr. Amy Cuddy" meaning believe in yourself and telling yourself you can do it. So, I applied—and I got the job.

My success in that role led to my current job at Koddi, a global leader in commerce media technology. Koddi's recruitment process involved taking a technical test in data analytics, and passing that was the final confirmation for me that yes, I really know what I'm doing. It was both a professional breakthrough and a personal breakthrough. Dr. McDaniel taught me that recognizing your worth is about knowing your value and presenting it with confidence. I may still turn to my power poses for that extra boost, but now I feel that I really know my worth.

Mariana's impressive career transition is a testament to the power we have when we believe that we *can*—that we deserve a seat at the table. Sometimes, we need someone else to pull out the seat for us, but ideally, we are able to march up to the table, pull out the chair ourselves, and sit in it confidently. Reaching that point mentally can take time, but there are things you can do to help reframe your mindset toward that end, such as:

- ✸ **Repeating mantras:** Have a go-to phrase you repeat to yourself. It can be as simple as "I can do this." Or, "I'm possible" (instead of impossible). This emphasizes the power of positive thinking and rejects self-limiting beliefs. If you tell yourself you can't do something, you're only defeating yourself. My grandfather used to say, "'Can't never' could do anything."

- ✸ **Learning new skills:** Challenge yourself by getting outside your comfort zone. This might mean learning a new language, taking on community service, or pursuing something that stretches your abilities. As you make progress, you'll see that you can do it.

- ✸ **Practicing creative pursuits:** Find something fun that opens up the creative side of your brain while shutting off negative stress. For me, painting has become a powerful tool—it's about mindset, growth, and finding joy while learning to be OK with imperfection.

- ✸ **Listening to podcasts or watching videos:** Focus on positive content that reinforces your ability to grow. I often listen to podcasts while painting, for example. If you're a more visual learner, you might prefer watching speeches on YouTube. For me, it has been a lot of Mel Robbins podcasts.

- ✸ **Journaling:** Write down your thoughts and progress to track your growth and build confidence over time. It only takes a few minutes of your day, and those few minutes can add up to hours of self-affirmation.

I think there are lots of different ways to build confidence, and different people have different approaches. I personally have never struggled much with imposter syndrome—I always felt drawn to go in certain directions and simply pursued that instinct. But at this point in my life, I'm making bigger and bolder moves than ever before, so my approach continues to evolve accordingly. The key is finding what works for you and remembering that growth happens when we step outside our comfort zones.

The Implications of Recognizing Your Worth

> *"Don't you dare shrink yourself for someone else's comfort. Do not become small for people who refuse to grow."* —Original source unknown

Recognizing self-worth has very practical implications. It's not just a question of feeling confident or liking what you see in that metaphorical mirror we discussed. Failing to fully appreciate your value can result not only in missed opportunities but also in giving away your power to others—something that can hold you back in your career and in life at large.

I once had to share an office space with a colleague who liked to work in a very warm environment, while I preferred a cooler one. I noticed that he would surreptitiously change the thermostat settings, nudging the temperature up and up and up. If you've ever had "The Great Thermostat Debate," be it with a colleague, family member, or friend, you know how passionate people can get about their preferred room temperature!

In this case, the thermostat debate was about more than temperature control. The gentleman also had a very authoritative approach toward me, both in terms of tone and action (for example, he would often talk over me). The thermostat was one symptom of a larger problem: someone wanting to take away my power. I knew that I had to address it without delay, and so I did, broaching the topic head-on. I respectfully listened to his rationale for wanting it so warm and then explained my own rationale for wanting it cooler before proposing a happy medium, which we both held to.

That might seem like a small thing, but I saw how it translated to other elements of the workplace. This gentleman continued to be pushy with other people—but he never was again with me because he knew that I wouldn't allow it. I knew my worth, and I knew what I deserved, and I wasn't going to let someone else cast doubt on that.

This attitude becomes especially important for those who want to rise to leadership positions in the professional world. When leaders show uncertainty or second-guess themselves, it makes others feel uncertain too. If you've ever had a boss who made a decision and then reneged on it, or who seemed to be incapable of making a decision at all, you know how unsettling it can be to have a doubt-ridden leader. I've witnessed this in my own career, when an organization I was working for welcomed a new leader with little experience. Their insecurity was palpable, and, unfortunately, it translated to a general culture of unease, as the uncertainty of leadership radiated to others.

When a different person stepped into that role with similarly limited leadership experience, there was a sense of nervous anticipation, as people worried that it would be the same story. However, this person took a different approach. They openly acknowledged that they didn't know what they didn't know. Instead of letting their inexperience rattle their confidence, they recognized it and took the time and care to learn about the environment, ask about existing issues, and then suggest solutions that were both well-informed and thoughtful. They didn't let their lack of leadership experience hinder them from acting like a leader. In short, they followed Amy Cuddy's advice: "Fake it till you become it." In the process, they became an excellent leader.

Whether in our professional or personal lives, this kind of growth requires recognizing our worth. But worth isn't just about knowing your value—it's about refusing to compromise when faced with the pressure to conform or diminish yourself. The following exercise can help you figure out where you're giving away your power and coach you on how to take it back, keeping you from shrinking yourself for another's comfort.

A Win-Win Exercise
Where Are You Giving Away Your Power?

Take a few minutes to reflect honestly on the following question: *Where am I giving away my power?* This isn't about blame or judgment—it's about awareness and reclaiming your agency.

Part 1: Reflection Questions

Consider these scenarios and ask yourself if any resonate.

In relationships (personal and professional):

1. Am I doing the majority of the work while others benefit?
2. Am I constantly seeking approval before making decisions?
3. Do I find myself "making it work," instead of letting it work naturally?
4. Do I find myself "keeping the peace" with others, instead of being honest and authentic?
5. Am I shrinking myself to make others comfortable?

In regard to perfectionism:

1. Am I giving too much power to the need for everything to be perfect?
2. Do I overanalyze decisions to the point of paralysis?
3. Am I exhausting myself trying to control every outcome?
4. Have I forgotten that "excellent" is awesome?

In professional settings:

1. Do I consistently undervalue my contributions in meetings or reviews?
2. Am I afraid to set boundaries with my colleagues or supervisors?
3. Do I downplay my experience or unique background?

Part 2: Action Steps

For each area where you identified giving away power, ask yourself, *What would it look like to reclaim this power?* What's one small step you can take this week to honor your worth in that situation?

Remember, sometimes you need to tell yourself, "I can do this." You deserve a seat at the table. Act like it!

Recognizing your self-worth isn't about ego. It's about accurately assessing your value so you can contribute most effectively, in a way that allows you to honor your full potential. Although others can remind us of our worth, it's primarily an internal process and is up to you to say, boldly and with conviction, "I can do it."

Self-Worth as the Foundation for Mental Resilience

> *"Your value does not decrease based on someone's inability to see your worth."* —Attributed to Olya Barnett

Ultimately, the true source of self-worth can only be yourself. While it's wonderful to surround yourself with cheerleaders, if you place too much value on the positive words of others, you're also more likely to place too much value on the negative words of others. The reality is that there will be naysayers, people who question your worth, and it's only by recognizing your value that you'll be able to stay true to your path regardless of who tries to discourage you.

I was listening to an interview with the CEO of Spanx, Sara Treleaven Blakely, who is one of the youngest self-made female billionaires.[2] In the talk, she revealed that she didn't tell anyone, even her husband, about her plans to create footless pantyhose for almost a whole year. She didn't want to risk someone saying something potentially negative about her idea and was adamant about protecting it from any negativity. I think that act of setting boundaries around what deserves your energy and attention can also be a way of recognizing your worth. And if you do share an idea, a plan, or a dream and someone says you *can't* do it, well … If you know your worth, you'll simply take that as a challenge and rise to the occasion to show them otherwise.

With self-worth, it's best to reframe setbacks as learning experiences rather than failures. It's also better to maintain a positive mindset—something many people find difficult—while staying

---

2   Talia Lakritz, "How Spanx Founder Sara Blakely Makes and Spends Her $1.1 Billion *Fortune," Business Insider,* February 22, 2024, https://www.businessinsider.com/spanx-sara-blakely-billionaire-net-worth-2024-2.

grounded and to make decisions and move forward without second-guessing yourself. And I believe a solid sense of self-worth also makes it easier to regulate your emotions, even as challenges arise. To me, all these things contribute to great mental resilience, a superpower we'll unpack in the next chapter.

CHAPTER 3

Developing Mental Resilience

"What do you consider your biggest failure?"

A graduate student asked me this question in the middle of a lecture. I was standing at the front of a classroom full of people, an adult version of the young girl who had once stood in front of a "classroom" of baby dolls and stuffed animals. By this point in my career, I was a confident educator and rarely became rattled, but this question gave me pause and prompted sincere reflection.

Have I made mistakes in my life? Absolutely. But I've never considered them failures or defeats. Rather, I view them as lessons to learn from, and some lessons were harder than others. Each has given me a deeper understanding of who I am, allowing me to align better with my authentic self and appreciate my own worth—and, in tandem, to build the kind of mental resilience and tenacity needed to make bold moves.

People commonly refer to their perspective on a glass of liquid as a barometer of their outlook. Is the glass half empty, or is it half full? Are you a pessimist or an optimist? I prefer a more nuanced approach and always say that the glass is refillable. It doesn't matter where that liquid level is now because you can always add more. This mindset that you always have the power to refill, restart, and rebuild is at the heart of mental resilience. It's the understanding that your past or current circumstances don't define your future capacity and that setbacks are simply opportunities to pour fresh energy and perspective into your life. This was my response to the question asked that day.

This philosophy was reinforced when I attended a class on authentic leadership at Harvard in 2017. We studied a book called *True North: Discover Your Authentic Leadership* by Bill George, with Peter Sims. It shared stories of CEOs who had lost their jobs or faced major setbacks only to discover that these apparent failures led them to their next—and often better—journey. The author posited that the key was not viewing these experiences as failures but as opportunities for growth and redirection. In short, the key was mindset.

This refillable glass approach is really about training your mind to be stronger than your emotions. It's recognizing that, in those moments when it might be tempting to give in to pessimism or fear, when the glass looks decidedly half empty, you can choose a different response. You can acknowledge that setbacks happen and then consciously decide to refill that glass. That's what this chapter will help you do: develop the mental tools and practices that allow you to respond to challenges with resilience rather than with emotion.

True Grit Goes Beyond Rose-Colored Glasses

"You gotta train your mind to be stronger than your emotions or else you'll lose yourself every time." —Original source unknown

Resilience is another one of those words that can be defined in many different ways, depending on who you ask. I personally prefer the term *tenacity*—or *grit*. To me, tenacity is about stripping away the emotionality that may instinctively arise when life throws you a curveball and simply keeping on. And life can throw all kinds of things your way. My mom is a very kind yet matter-of-fact woman, and even when I was a girl, she used to tell me, "Life isn't always fair. Life is hard." That simple fact was ingrained in me from an early age: Life isn't fair, so don't cry about it, don't dwell on it, just take your next step, and keep on moving.

That mindset was complemented by the wise words of my grandfather, who liked to say, "'Can't never' could do anything." Those words speak to the fact that tenacity is above all a mindset. While you can't always change your situation, you can change how you frame and react to it, and that can make all the difference in how high you rise above it.

All this became clear to me through my work with student athletes. I spent part of my academic career also serving as the FAR, a role that had me reporting directly to the chancellor while serving as a liaison between the faculty, student athletes, and athletics administration. I interacted with a lot of athletes in that capacity, and the pressure some of these young people were under was astounding. If they missed a kick, they might lose the game. If they dropped a pass, they might let down their coach, their teammates, or the fans. With social media, news media, sports outlets, and TV, millions of people would know about a missed field goal or a missed foul shot within minutes. While some athletes did not come through under pressure, those who did were the ones who shone.

In sports and in life, when you start enjoying the process, you often do better, simply because the enjoyment relieves some of the pressure you're putting on yourself. This shift of focus from outcome to process is fundamentally about changing where you direct your mental energy. Reframing your mindset to focus on process rather than problem allows you to channel your energy into what you can control—your effort, your approach, and your growth—instead of worrying about things outside your influence.

Sometimes, that shift in mindset can be as simple as a shift in language. I've coached a lot of people who have anxiety around board of director meetings, job interviews, presentations, and public speaking, and I always advise them to reframe nervousness as excitement. When they're in front of a room of people, they might notice physical signs of nerves, such as a racing heart rate, flushed cheeks, and sweaty palms. However, these physical signs can also be indicators of another emotion: excitement. After drawing this parallel, I tell my coaching clients that I never want to hear the word *nervous* from them again—and ask them to replace this word with *excited* when they talk about public speaking. Instead of saying, "I'm nervous about my presentation," they say, "I'm excited about my presentation." We both know what they really mean—there are invisible air quotes around *excited* as they say it—but it's nonetheless a small step toward reframing the experience and building resilience.

That's not to say that tenacity means everything is sunshine, rainbows, and roses. It's not about blind optimism. In fact, wearing rose-colored glasses insistently at all times can backfire. I remember once meeting a woman who was just a ray of sunshine—nice, energetic, optimistic—*all the time*. At some point, I had the thought, *Nobody can be this happy all of the time*. Eventually, I learned that this woman was experiencing some very serious issues in her personal life. It turned out that her sunshiny personality was largely a coping mechanism, a way of avoiding the difficult work of addressing her problems. She had chosen to paint over reality with forced positivity instead of building true tenacity.

True tenacity happens when you take in the good and the bad and keep moving anyway. It's not glamorous. It's just about putting one foot in front of the other. I think that defines some of the most successful people we encounter in life. Legendary Tennessee basketball coach Pat Summitt writes about her secret to success in her book, summing it up thusly: "Here's how I'm going to beat you: I'm going to outwork you. That's it. That's all there is to it. You just learned my most valuable secret. It's not that exciting."[3]

This is the essence of tenacity—it's not flashy or dramatic. It's the quiet determination to keep showing up, to keep working, to keep refilling that glass no matter how many times it gets knocked over. It's about consistency and intensity. And it's about understanding that grit doesn't live in a vacuum but requires us to navigate relationships with and feedback from others, and admittedly, that is where things can get tricky.

Resilience Beyond the Individual

> *"Grit is passion and perseverance for very long-term goals."*
> —Angela Duckworth

Resilience allows you to see clearly while reacting logically and authentically. That can serve you well in any facet of life, personally or professionally. It will not only allow you to manage emotions and keep moving in the face of setbacks but also to take on feedback in a meaningful way without doing damage to your sense of self-worth—a delicate balancing act.

The topic of feedback raises an important point that I think is relevant to any discussion of resilience: the fact that it relates to other people beyond ourselves. Some approaches to resilience suggest that it comes from a stoic attitude: being able to have anything thrown at you and letting it roll off your back. Based on my experiences as

---

3   Pat Summitt, *Reach for the Summit: The Definite Dozen System for Succeeding at Whatever You Do* (Crown Currency, 1999).

an educator, mentor, colleague, and coach, I don't think it's quite so simple. True resilience requires not just understanding and managing your own emotions but also recognizing the emotions and motivations of those around you.

One of the most obvious examples of this is handling critique. I was always taught to use the sandwich approach when delivering a critique: You start with something positive, then address the issue and talk about how it can be resolved, and finally, end with a positive. However, critique is not always delivered in such a judicious manner. And in some cases, depending on one's perception, a comment or action that isn't even intended as a critique can be taken as such.

The truth is that if something really triggers us, it's rarely about the other person; it's often because, deep down, we recognize a grain of truth in what they said. It's not about the message delivery or the messenger—it's about the message, and when we are triggered by the message, it usually means it touched something in us. The trick isn't about getting thicker skin; it's about developing a better filter and recognizing that a *well-intentioned* critique can be a learning opportunity—a chance to add some liquid to your glass.

When I used to grade papers as an educator, I'd use what I called my "red pen of caring," reassuring students that my scribbles on their papers were not meant to discourage them but to build them up. I'd tell them, "Don't panic when you see the red lines! Read the comments, we'll talk about how to fix things, and maybe you can earn some points back on your grade for this paper." With that possibility of additional points, I gave them the chance to add some liquid to their glass, if you will.

I took a similar approach myself when going through the rigorous process to become tenured as an academic, framing the comments that were given to me as opportunities to "earn some points back."

When I received feedback from department committees, college committees, and deans, I could have gotten frustrated—and sometimes I did, initially. But instead of sitting around thinking, *This isn't fair*, I decided to address every single point of feedback I received.

The next year, I would make sure my cover letter clearly stated, "Thank you for your advice last year. You advised me to do *X*. Here's what I did to address each point. You can find the documentation on page *Y* of my binder." By the time I got to my final tenure year evaluation, I had compiled two five-inch binders of documentation that became known as the gold standard for the department. Did I take it a little too far? Maybe. But I was respectful, thorough, and systematic in responding to feedback.

The way up the career ladder is usually full of feedback, so anyone looking to get to the top would do well to learn how to take it gracefully. Even executives are subject to feedback loops such as 360 reviews. Feedback is something that you'll experience at every stage of your career, so it's worth taking the time to figure out how to handle it now.

Understanding how different behavioral styles process emotions can also enhance your resilience when working with others. In my work with DISC behavioral assessments, I've observed that people with task-oriented styles (dominance and conscientiousness) tend to stick more closely to the tasks when emotions run high, while those with people-oriented styles (influence and steadiness) are more likely to lead with their feelings. This isn't to say that task-oriented people don't have emotions—they absolutely do—but they're less likely to wear those feelings on their sleeve. A conversation between two task-oriented people about a difficult issue will probably focus on problem-solving. When that conversation is between two people-oriented individuals, emotions may flare more readily. The real challenge comes when you have one of each type trying to communicate. Understanding these differences allows you to adjust your approach, acknowledging feelings when working with people-oriented colleagues and focusing on facts and solutions with task-oriented team members. This awareness doesn't just help you give feedback more effectively—it also helps you receive it with greater resilience, because you can recognize that someone's delivery style may be more about their communication preferences than about their intentions toward you.

When someone gives you specific suggestions, it then becomes easier to see their feedback not as criticism meant to tear you down but as a growth opportunity—reframing the situation as a chance to refill your glass with new knowledge and improved performance. The following exercises can help you develop these mental resilience skills through daily practice.

A Win-Win Exercise
Building Tenacity and Resilience

Developing tenacity and resilience takes time—these traits are developed through consistent daily practices that train your mind to respond rather than react. This exercise combines morning mindset practices with trigger awareness to help you build lasting mental strength.

Part 1: Morning Mindset Prep

Before you get out of bed each morning, take a moment to set your mental tone for the day. Instead of letting your mind immediately jump to stresses or problems, deliberately choose your first thoughts. Replace thoughts like, *Oh no, I have to deal with [difficult situation] today* or *This is going to be a stressful day* or *I'm dreading [specific meeting/task]* with intentional affirmations, such as:

1. *This is going to be a great day for [specific opportunity].*
2. *I am prepared to handle whatever comes my way today.*
3. *I choose to approach today's challenges with calm confidence.*
4. *I am awesome.*

Part 2: The Midday Emotional Reset

When you feel emotions starting to flare during the day, pause and count down slowly: five, four, three, two, one (and, if you need an extra beat, add a zero) … And then let the emotion pass. Remember, emotions are temporary. Pause before responding and choose your response with logic and facts rather than pure emotion.

Part 3: Evening Trigger Identifier

Reflect on your day to identify the moments when you felt triggered. Complete these sentences honestly, taking time to think about your responses. While I've included work-relevant phrases, these can be adapted to personal contexts as well:

1. What do people do that makes me frustrated?
2. What offends me most at work?
3. What behavior do I find most offensive?
4. What is the most annoying phrase I hear?
5. What actions make me irritated?

For each trigger you identified, ask yourself:

1. What specifically about this situation bothers me?
2. Is this trigger based on facts, emotions, or my interpretation?
3. How can I pause and respond rather than react when this happens?
4. What would a mentally resilient response look like in this situation?

Finally, with your own triggers identified, extend that awareness to others. Consider the triggers of your teammates and colleagues. The more aware you are of what sets yourself and others off, the better you can communicate and collaborate.

Practice this exercise for one week, and notice how your mental tenacity and resilience grow when you're proactive about managing your mindset and emotional responses.

When you approach it with the right mindset, other people's feedback can become a means of fueling you. It's about how you frame it. You always have a choice in how you interpret and respond to what others say—that choice is where your power lies.

Tenacity and Resilience: The Key to Professional Stamina

> *"We don't grow when things are easy; we grow when we face challenges."* —Attributed to Joyce Meyer

Tenacity and resilience combined are a kind of superpower. For leaders, these qualities are particularly critical. The adage that "it's lonely at the top" does hold true in some ways: A leader must remain the calm captain in any storm and can't bring high-level concerns to their employees. If a junior employee has a bad day at work, they might join their colleagues at the bar afterward to debrief and unwind. For a CEO, this isn't a realistic option. One-on-one leadership coaching, which provides both guidance and confidentiality, can be one way for leaders to get feedback and build their tenacity and resilience.

With that said, these traits are relevant to all of us, not only leaders—and they're essential beyond the workplace as well, as they give us the mental stamina necessary to weather life's storms. Mental stamina isn't just about toughing it out; it's about developing the capacity to bounce back stronger. It can help protect not only the mind but also the body. There is now a significant body of research that links conditions such as stress to an array of mental and physical health problems, from depression to an increased risk of cardiovascular disease.[4] Knowing that, nurturing tenacity and resilience becomes an essential act of self-care for both mind and body—the kind of foundational self-care that goes beyond surface-level comfort to build lasting strength.

This kind of self-care follows the same principle as the oxygen mask on an airplane: You've got to put on your own mask first before you can effectively help others with theirs. In the next chapter, we'll consider what that oxygen mask might look like for different types of people and why it's so critical.

---

4   Eberhard Fuchs and Gabriele Flügge, "Cellular Consequences of Stress and Depression," *Dialogues in Clinical Neuroscience* 6, no. 2 (2004): 171–83, https://doi.org/10.31887/DCNS.2004.6.2/efuchs; Andrew Steptoe and Mika Kivimäki, "Stress and Cardiovascular Disease," *Nature Reviews Cardiology* 9 (2012): 360–70, https://doi.org/10.1038/nrcardio.2012.45.

CHAPTER 4

Put Your Oxygen Mask on First

We all need a way to mentally unplug—to pause, breathe, and slow the constant whir of our minds. For me, that way is painting. I picked up the hobby in my late forties. Am I going to be the next Picasso, Van Gogh, or Monet? No. I prefer paint-by-numbers scenes that are ready-made for me, allowing me to tune out while I fill them in, bit by bit, one brushstroke at a time.

Painting allows me to quiet the logical, practical part of my brain and tap into the more creative side. I often use this time for brainstorming ideas. Other times, I'll paint while I listen to a podcast that educates, motivates, or inspires me. The practice is deeply soothing, and I can think of no better way to spend a rainy evening than in front of a canvas, brush in hand, my cats curled up nearby.

My painting serves another purpose as well: manifestation. I often paint scenes of Italy, a place I'd like to travel to one day. As visions of Venetian canals, the craggy cliffs of the Cinque Terre, the vineyards of Tuscany, or the Colosseum of Rome arise before me, I can picture myself there, glass of wine in hand, a plate of pasta before me. I'm not there physically yet, but I will be—someday. My paintings are both a manifestation and a promise.

The practice of painting also teaches me to let go in some ways. I believe in pursuing perfection, knowing that excellence comes along the way. Painting reassures me that excellence is quite all right—perfection isn't a must. Got some paint outside of the lines? That's OK. Mixed up a couple colors? Fine; it makes a beautiful new color. In the end, it's still going to be a beautiful piece of art that I can enjoy, my way.

Painting has enriched my life, not just as a hobby but as a form of self-improvement. It is one of my oxygen masks: something I reach for when I am feeling stressed or overwhelmed and need to press pause. And I have no doubt that the soothing effect it has on me benefits my mind, my body, and my spirit.

We all need an oxygen mask in life. It's important for anyone, at any stage and phase, professionally and personally. It's especially important for leaders, who tend to have an even greater burden of responsibility than most and, with it, greater stress. In this context, it becomes even more important to, as they always tell you on an airplane, put your own mask on first before helping others.

It sounds easy in theory, but in practice, it can be difficult. Maybe it makes you feel selfish to take care of your own needs first. Or maybe it's been so long since you did that you aren't even sure what it looks like. This chapter helps elucidate just why it's so important to put your own oxygen mask on first and then helps you answer the question: What does *your* oxygen mask look like?

The Science Behind the Oxygen Mask: Why Self-Care Isn't Selfish

"I told my friend that I'm emotionally hitting a wall, and she said, 'Sometimes walls are there so we can lean on them and rest.'"

—Attributed to Brandon Kyle Goodman[5]

I picked up painting shortly after my father was given a cancer diagnosis. Perhaps it was a time when I needed an oxygen mask more than usual, and it proved so effective that I still continue to reach for it, even now that my father is in good health. Throughout my father's illness, I was eager to support him and my mom as much as possible.

The diagnosis came shortly after I'd made the bold move to leave academia and start my first corporate job, working for a global talent advisory firm. While the role did allow for some remote flexibility, which allowed me to be with my parents more, it was also a new challenge—and very stressful. I often felt like I was trying to drink water from a fire hydrant as I sought to excel in my new role, support my parents, and travel back and forth between work and my parents' home.

As an only child, I took the role of supporting my parents on their healthcare journey very seriously. I had to push my dad to get diagnosed, and when the results came in, I was the one who conveyed the news and what it meant. I knew the type of cancer suspected was very aggressive and that time was of the essence, so I also insisted that he go to a high-quality healthcare facility.

Although I tried to help as much as I could, it was my mother who was my father's primary caregiver, and she went above and beyond

---

5   Brandon Kyle Goodman (@brandonkgood), "I told my friend that I'm emotionally 'hitting a wall' and she said 'Sometimes walls are there so we can lean on them and rest.' I can't even begin to express how much I really needed to hear that.," Twitter (now X), January 17, 2021, https://x.com/brandonkgood/status/1350837356073414657.

in that role. I believe that my mom's care was a big part of the reason why my father never needed a feeding tube, something that's quite common for throat cancer patients. She worked tirelessly to take care of him, and her dedication and tenacity were evident—but it did take an emotional and physical toll on her. She is one strong woman and has taught me so many things in life.

Caregiver stress is something I was keenly aware of well before my father's illness—I'd researched it extensively for my PhD dissertation, which examined organizational support mechanisms for employees managing traumatic caregiving responsibilities and drew parallels between caregiver stress and employee turnover, commitment, and job satisfaction in the workplace.[6] The negative impacts of caregiver stress elucidated in my dissertation include but are not limited to:

- ⚙ Job-related consequences, including increased family–work conflict, psychological strain, and decreased job satisfaction and organizational commitment.

- ⚙ Mental and physical health effects, with one in three caregivers rating their health as fair to poor. Common issues include depression, anxiety, sleep disturbances, eating disorders, and physical illnesses.[7] Caregivers also often experience emotional exhaustion and detachment from their jobs.[8]

- ⚙ High burnout risk, especially when caregivers continue working out of financial or insurance-related necessity.

---

6   Karen McDaniel, "Exploring Organizational Support Mechanisms to Reduce Affects of Traumatic Caregiver Stress" (PhD diss., University of Memphis, 2008).

7   *Caregiver Stress and Health* (National Women's Health Information Center, 2003).

8   Christina Maslach, "A Multidimensional Theory of Burnout," in *Theories of Organizational Stress*, ed. Cary L. Cooper (Oxford University Press, 1998), 68–85.

In my research, parallels to leadership dynamics became evident. Just as caregivers who neglect their own needs ultimately become less effective at caring for others, leaders who neglect self-care become less effective at leading their teams. When you're running on empty—whether from caregiver stress or leadership pressure—you have nothing left to offer others. It's the oxygen mask principle in action.

Running on empty can also increase the risk of burnout. In recent years, burnout has become more widely recognized, and has even been identified as an occupational phenomenon in the *International Classification of Diseases 11th Revision*, the global health information standard developed and maintained by the World Health Organization.[9] Knowing this, it becomes even more important that we all have an oxygen mask to reach for—and that we don't hesitate to reach for it when we need it. It's not selfish to put your own mask on first. And it doesn't have to be complicated. Sometimes, it's as simple as saying no to reclaim some time for yourself.

Pressing Pause: The Ultimate Oxygen Mask

"There are two types of tired: one that requires rest, and one that requires peace." –Original source unknown

I'm the type of person who likes to keep busy. My family used to tease me that my plate was full and I needed to remove a thing or two from it. I didn't really listen. Instead, I kept adding things to my plate, to the point that they said, "Fine, we're just going to have to get you a platter!"

---

9   "Burn-Out an 'Occupational Phenomenon': International Classification of Diseases," World Health Organization, May 28, 2019, https://www.who.int/news/item/28-05-2019-burn-out-an-occupational-phenomenon-international-classification-of-diseases.

Inevitably, my platter started overflowing. I finally had to press pause and tell myself, "Stop." I recognized that I had overloaded myself with obligations, and as much as I may have enjoyed them, I was on the brink of crashing. A friend told me to get control of my calendar.

We might find ourselves overloaded in life for all kinds of reasons. Sometimes, it comes from internal pressure. Other times, it comes from outside pressure, from bosses to well-intentioned friends and family. If that pressure is left unchecked, it can build and build, having disastrous effects on our mental, emotional, and physical well-being.

Ideally, you will be able to recognize that your plate is getting too full before it gets so overloaded that you have no choice but to let it go crashing to the floor. That metaphorical crash can show itself in a lot of different ways, from health problems to missed deadlines.

One of the most important things anyone can do to avoid overloading their plate is to master the art of saying no—a word that demands pause. Sometimes, people don't even recognize that they've been saying yes to things when they should really be saying no. That's why I like to share these five warning signs that can help you identify when you're saying yes but mean no:[10]

- ✿ You regret saying yes immediately after having done so.

- ✿ You cancel commitments later.

- ✿ You feel resentful after agreeing to something.

- ✿ You prioritize keeping the peace with a yes over meeting your own needs with a no.

- ✿ You feel the need to say yes to avoid disappointing others (or the guilt it may incite).

---

10   Sunita Sah, *Defy: The Power of No in a World That Demands Yes* (Random House, 2025).

No is a very powerful word that can help us create the pause we need not only to assess how full our plate is but also to actually take care of ourselves. The basic things, such as eating well and sleeping enough, often tend to go out the window if we're saying yes to everything. When we're constantly keeping busy, it's also tricky to recognize burnout creeping up on us. Pressing pause, taking a big gulp of oxygen, and reflecting for a moment on how we're feeling can be the first step toward recognizing the early warning signs of burnout. These can include[11]

- feelings of frustration or irritability,

- a sense of detachment,

- lack of energy or fatigue,

- an inability to concentrate, and/or

- reduced standards at work.

When these things start to creep up on you, it's a good indicator that your plate is too full. That said, for ambitious individuals, achieving a healthy work–life integration isn't always easy. Leaders, in particular, may struggle to strike the right balance. It's also important to note that everybody's version of what's healthy in terms of work–life integration is different. Some people can handle more than others, and people perceive and cope with stress differently. The key is to find your own sense of balance, one that fits your unique needs—and to then hold yourself accountable to what you can and cannot take on. I've included a personal oxygen audit that you can use to check in with yourself.

---

11   "How to Recognise the Warning Signs of Burn Out," British Medical Association, April 30, 2025, https://www.bma.org.uk/news-and-opinion/how-to-recognise-the-warning-signs-of-burn-out.

A Win-Win Exercise
Your Personal Oxygen Audit

Taking care of yourself isn't selfish—it's essential for sustainable leadership and authentic living. This exercise helps you identify what's depleting your oxygen supply and what practices can help you breathe freely again.

Part 1: Oxygen Audit

Take an honest look at your daily life and identify your oxygen drains and sources. What energizes you versus what drains you? Sometimes what's draining you isn't what you think it is—it might be internal pressure you're putting on yourself rather than just external circumstances.

Oxygen Drains

What's depleting your oxygen tank levels? Rate each area on a scale of one to five (one being minimal drain, five being a major drain):

1. Work responsibilities and deadlines
2. Difficult relationships or conflicts (especially conflict avoidance)
3. Financial concerns
4. Health issues or lack of self-care
5. Perfectionism and self-criticism
6. Saying yes when you mean no
7. Cluttered or disorganized environment
8. Negative self-talk
9. Social obligations that don't align with your values
10. Technology overload / constant connectivity

Oxygen Sources

What fills up your oxygen tank? Rate each area on a scale of one to five (one being minimal energy, five being an energizer):

1. Meaningful work or projects
2. Quality time with loved ones
3. Physical exercise or movement
4. Creative activities
5. Time in nature
6. Learning something new
7. Helping others
8. Spiritual practices or meditation
9. Hobbies that bring you joy
10. Taking a walk
11. Quiet time for reflection

Review your energy audit. What patterns do you notice? What small changes could you make to reduce your energy drains or increase your energy sources? Use this exercise regularly to check in with yourself and ask, "How are my oxygen levels?"

Remember: Putting on your oxygen mask first isn't about being selfish—it's about ensuring you have the energy and clarity to show up authentically for yourself and others. Start small, be consistent, and be kind to yourself as you build these practices.

One of the most powerful oxygen masks we have is free and available to us every single morning: our self-talk. The National Science Foundation found that people have sixty thousand thoughts per day, with 80 percent of those being negative and 95 percent being repetitive.[12] We're basically running the same negative mental loops over and over again. This is why the way we start our day matters so much.

---

12   Julia Burket, "22 Facts About the Brain: World Brain Day," DENT Neurologic Institute, accessed June 20, 2025, https://www.dentinstitute. com/22-facts-about-the-brain-world-brain-day.

If you're waking up thinking, *I dread this day, I hate going to work,* or *I don't want to have this conversation today,* your trajectory for the day is negative. That's why, every morning before I get out of bed, I tell myself, *This is going to be a great day.* And if I don't really mean it or feel it, I'll say it again with more authority. The goal is to tell my brain that, whatever happens—even if it's hard—everything is working together for the greater good. This isn't about rose-colored glasses positivity or pretending challenges don't exist. It's about choosing to approach your day from a place of possibility rather than dread.

Of course, an oxygen mask should go beyond self-talk. And in that respect, everyone's oxygen mask looks different. For me, spending time around other people is one way of refilling my tank with O2. That doesn't mean it has to be your way. Some people gain energy from solitude. Some people are able to mentally reset while sitting in stillness. Others need to be on the go. And the things that really bring us peace, not just rest (be it gardening, reading, dancing, etc.), vary according to the individual. Taking the time now to identify those things will serve you later, in all aspects of life.

As a natural extrovert who thrives on interaction and movement, I initially found it challenging to embrace quieter forms of restoration. However, discovering painting taught me the value of cultivating what I call "creativity and innovation"—those moments of focused solitude that spark creativity and deeper reflection. This balance has proven especially valuable in my speaking and leadership work, where the ability to draw from both energizing social connections and contemplative inner work creates a more authentic and sustainable approach to serving others.

Understanding your natural tendencies while also developing complementary skills creates a more extensive tool kit for managing stress and maintaining peak performance, especially when the demands of leadership require you to show up consistently for your team.

The Gateway to Better Communication

"Don't be so busy that you miss out on life." –Original source unknown

People have different oxygen masks because people are different. What's restorative to one person may be stressful to another. These aren't just preferences; they reflect deeper differences in how we process information, make decisions, and communicate with others. The irony is that when we're always on the go, running from meeting to meeting, project to project, or crisis to crisis, we often miss the subtle cues that reveal these differences in the people around us, assuming that others operate the way we do without taking the time to recognize how they *really* operate—which may be very different from us.

This can lead to misunderstandings, friction, and missed opportunities for connection, both personally and professionally. If we instead slow down long enough to hit the pause button, the ultimate oxygen mask, we create the mental space to understand others. That's when we might realize that the colleague who seems abrasive might just have a different communication style, or the friend who's distant might simply recharge in a different way than we like to.

Understanding these differences and learning to adapt our communication accordingly isn't just about being more effective at work. It's about not missing out on the richness that comes from connecting with others, both in the workplace and outside of it. The next chapter examines how we can better understand ourselves and those around us and then use that knowledge to adapt our communication. By exploring different personality types and communication styles—starting with tools such as the DISC profiles—we can learn to speak others' languages rather than expecting them to speak ours. After all, life is happening in those interactions, and we want to make the most of each one.

Connection

Building Effective Relationships

CHAPTER 5

The Art of Effective Communication

Learning a new language is difficult. Back when I was in academia, I had such admiration for my international students, who not only learned a new language but also experienced a new culture in coming to the United States. I got a sense for how overwhelming this could be in a fun exercise I first participated in as part of my own MBA studies: the BaFá BaFá exercise created by Dr. R. Garry Shirts.

The exercise begins by sending a few people out of the room. While they're gone, the remaining group learns a made-up "beta language" with invented words and gestures. When the excluded participants return, they must figure out how to communicate and complete a simple task using only this unfamiliar language system—no English allowed. The confusion and awkwardness they experience trying to navigate this completely foreign communication system mirror how disorienting it can be to enter a new culture and understand a new language. Through this process, the participants learn flexibility and adaptability, empathy, and tolerance for ambiguity. They also get a sense of what it's like to interact with a foreign language and culture.

That moment of stepping into the room, unsure of the rules, the language, or how you'll be perceived, highlights a universal truth about communication: The way we present ourselves before we speak often sets the tone for everything that follows. Whether you're navigating an unfamiliar language or simply entering a meeting, those first few moments carry tremendous weight.

It takes five seconds to make a first impression. Communication starts with the first impression—and technically, it begins before you even open your mouth. If you slouch into a room with a scowl and a storm cloud hanging over you, you will probably be received pretty differently than if you walk in with your head held high and a smile on your face. The way that you hold yourself, the way that you introduce yourself, your attire, your confidence—everything is wrapped into that first impression, and it's hard to recover from a bad one. You never get a second chance to make a first impression.

When I coach business leaders, they're often surprised by how much emphasis I place on etiquette in first impressions. They expect to jump right into communication issues, such as how to negotiate or deliver tough feedback. However, I always take time to teach some basic professional etiquette as part of any communication coaching.

For example, in some cultures, it's considered rude to take a business card with one hand only—and even ruder to not even glance at it as you take it. Once I learned this, I started presenting and receiving business cards with two hands and always taking a moment to glance at the ones I was given. It's not disrespectful here in the United States, and it shows cultural awareness when I'm working with international colleagues.

Paying careful attention to a business card has another benefit—it helps you remember the person's name. As you receive a card with two hands, you can look at the name on it, then look up and connect the name with the face. Then you can look back down at the card and say something like, "John, it was such a pleasure meeting you today." If you repeat a name three times during the course of your initial interaction, it helps you remember it later—and remembering names is important, as it makes people feel seen, which is exactly the kind of first impression you want to leave as a leader.

Of course, you can make the greatest first impression in the world, but if you then go on to communicate in a way that isn't well received by the other party, even the best first impression in the world can't save you. The tricky thing is that people are all so fundamentally different. What seems like an acceptable or normal communication pattern to one person might not be interpreted as such by another. For example, someone who speaks loudly and is outspoken might be seen as rude or overbearing by someone who is quiet and reticent.

Luckily, there is a tool that can help crack the code in how we communicate—and it's one I use regularly with my coaching clients. I've alluded to it a few times already in this book, but this chapter on communication is where I really want to unpack it: the DISC profile.

Understanding Communication Styles Through DISC

> *"Most people do not listen with the intent to understand; they listen with the intent to reply."* –Stephen Covey[13]

DISC is one pathway to developing emotional intelligence (EI), which is critical for effective communication. EI isn't about suppressing feelings but channeling them toward understanding, as it requires you to be aware of both your own and others' emotions. A part of EI is also recognizing your own strengths and weaknesses—something DISC helps you do—as well as your triggers, something we discussed in the previous chapter (see the win-win exercise in chapter 3).

---

13   Stephen R. Covey, *The 7 Habits of Highly Effective People: Restoring the Character Ethic* (Free Press, 2004).

Here is a very high-level overview of each of these four styles and their communication preferences:

- **Dominance ("my way"):** People with high *D* traits are fast-paced, task oriented, and direct. They're results driven, competitive, and motivated by getting things done. They tend to be quick decision-makers who focus on challenges and bottom-line results.

  - When communicating with *D* styles, be clear, brief, and specific—get to the point quickly, and don't ramble.

- **Influence ("the fun way"):** High-*I* individuals are people oriented, enthusiastic, and entertaining. They're optimistic, talkative, and motivated by social acceptance and recognition. They love to engage with others and tend to be inspiring team members.

  - When communicating with *I* styles, allow time for socializing, listen actively, ask questions, and give them positive feedback.

- **Steadiness ("the peaceful way"):** Those with high *S* characteristics are relationship focused and consensus seeking. They're dependable, patient, supportive, and motivated by security and stability. They prefer predictable environments and are excellent listeners who resist sudden changes.

  - When communicating with *S* styles, slow down, allow time for them to process their thoughts, be sincere, and give them time to make decisions.

- **Conscientiousness ("the right way"):** High-*C* people are detail oriented, accurate, and analytical. They're precise, cautious, and motivated by being right and having complete information. They tend to be systematic thinkers who focus on quality and procedure.

- When communicating with C styles, be organized, have your facts prepared, be straightforward, and give them the data they need to make informed decisions.

These differences can impact how people converse and collaborate in a big way. Let's say a high D and a high C are working together on a project. According to the DISC manual, this pairing has the lowest communication effectiveness because while both styles are task oriented, they clash on decision speed and risk orientation. The high D is risk seeking and ready to move forward with minimal data, while the high C is risk averse and wants comprehensive information before making any decisions. The D gets frustrated with what they see as the C's slow pace and overanalysis, while the C views the D as reckless and pushy.

However, once they become aware of these differences, they can adapt their communication styles and become a fantastic team. The D learns to slow down and provide more detailed information, recognizing that the C's thoroughness prevents costly mistakes. The C learns to set analysis deadlines and provide executive summaries, understanding that the D's urgency captures important opportunities. This awareness transforms potential conflict into complementary strengths—the D's drive for results combined with the C's data focus creates solutions that are both timely and well researched.

DISC can serve many purposes, but if I had to boil it down to a single sentence, I'd say it's all about knowing and controlling yourself while understanding others and adapting where appropriate. In helping you do this, DISC can help you get to the win-wins—something we'll look at in greater detail in later chapters.

Tips for Applying DISC

> *"The most important thing in communication is hearing what isn't said."* –Attributed to Peter F. Drucker

I've experienced for myself how an understanding of DISC can help minimize friction and improve communication and collaboration. I was once working with a colleague on a project, and our first meeting was a perfect example of how different styles can clash when you don't adjust your approach.

I'm naturally energetic, direct, and to the point, so I went into my colleague's office with a sheet of paper outlining three clear points. He was leading the project, and I knew he was very busy, so I didn't want to take up a lot of his time.

After some brief pleasantries, I got to it and laid out the three points we needed to discuss: "Here's point one, point two, point three." Again, in light of how busy he was (as was I), I prioritized efficiency: "For point one, we could do this. For point two, what if we handle it that way? For point three, what do you think?"

After I'd laid it all out, he just sat there for a moment before finally responding, "OK, let me think about it."

Initially, I perceived this as positive—but when I tried to steer the conversation back to the matter at hand, seeking concrete answers, he demurred and changed the subject yet again. In the end, we didn't get anything done, and I left the meeting feeling confused. I had come in prepared and ready to make decisions. Why couldn't we move forward and get things done?

Upon reflection, I realized that we had completely opposite behavioral styles. He seemed to be a very steady individual—from what I knew of him, he was someone who was very relational and needed to slow things down.

When we had our follow-up meeting, I had the same piece of paper with the three points, but I completely changed my approach. I went in and said, "How are you today? What happened over the weekend with that event in town? Were you there? Did your daughter go with you? How is she, by the way?" I slowed down and took the time to talk about more relational things.

Only once that was done did we get to the reason I was there: the three points on my sheet of paper. Even then, I approached things differently from in that first meeting. Instead of telling him the three points and providing proposals with direct feedback requests, I kept my questions more open-ended, focusing on "how" questions. "How do you think we should handle this? How do you think or feel about that? How would you advise that we approach this?" I was giving him more time by asking open-ended questions instead of just making statements and expecting a quick response.

The meeting took probably at least twice as long. But since he was leading the project, it was important to accommodate his style. Once I did that, we made a dynamic team. After that meeting, we learned each other's strengths and weaknesses, and we developed a really good working relationship. We got on the same page, understood each other's differences, and figured out how we could complement each other as a team instead of being two people in separate roles trying to accomplish something. That's how DISC led us to several win-wins over the years we worked together.

Realistically, you can't ask everyone you interact with in life to complete a DISC assessment. However, you can get a sense for someone's style in your interactions with them and then adapt accordingly. This anecdote demonstrates how understanding behavioral differences can help with unproductive or difficult conversations and turn them into fruitful collaborations. Here are some key communication strategies that can help you navigate these differences more effectively.

RECOGNIZE THE VALUE OF QUESTIONS VERSUS STATEMENTS

Some DISC styles, such as mine, naturally collect information and want to share it with everyone. When I see someone facing a challenge, my instinct is to help by giving them all the knowledge I've gathered on the topic. While my intentions are good—I'm not trying to be a know-it-all—my approach can come across as overwhelming, especially to someone whose style doesn't appreciate that level of intensity and information all at once.

I've learned the power of asking questions instead of making statements. Now I start by asking, "Are you interested in learning more about this topic?" If they say yes, I follow up with, "I've studied this a lot. How much information would you like?" This lets them tell me what they can handle.

REMOVE JUDGMENTS

Beyond the physical environment, we must also consider the emotional environment that each person brings to every interaction. People have different attachment styles, varying stress levels, and may be dealing with circumstances we know nothing about. You might be looking at someone who is smiling, but you don't know what's behind that smile—they could be dealing with family issues, health concerns, or work pressures that are affecting their ability to communicate effectively. This is why it's so important to remove judgment and listen to understand, not just to respond. When we approach conversations with curiosity rather than assumptions, we create space for authentic communication and genuine connection.

BE EMPATHETIC—TO YOURSELF AS WELL

Effective communication isn't about suppressing feelings but channeling them toward understanding. That means understanding others—but also yourself. You also need to understand your triggers and what puts you under stress because that's when communication often breaks down. It's important to practice self-compassion when you make mistakes or speak too harshly under pressure—you're human, you get stressed, and you have emotions. You aren't a robot, and sometimes you have to ease up on yourself rather than beating yourself up, which only makes things worse.

LOOK AT NONVERBAL CUES

Paying attention to body language is crucial, as so much of communication happens through nonverbal cues. Noticing someone's body language gives you a richer context for what someone is really trying to communicate. If someone says they are at ease, but their arms are crossed and their shoulders are hunched, are they really at ease? If someone says they're fine, but they are avoiding eye contact and speaking in clipped tones, are they really OK? Sometimes, people don't even realize they are not at ease. It's often said that the most important thing in communication is hearing what isn't said—and I'd say that holds true.

CONSIDER ENVIRONMENTAL FACTORS

Finally, the physical environment plays a bigger role in communication than most people realize. I remember when, in my first couple of years teaching, we had a classroom with broken air-conditioning and a heat-producing projector that made the room unbearably hot. Students were distracted, uncomfortable, and less engaged—not because they didn't care about the material but because the environment was working against effective communication. Temperature, lighting, noise levels, and even seating arrangements can all impact how well people can focus and participate in meaningful dialogue.

Recognizing influences such as the environment—coupled with understanding your communication style and recognizing the styles of others—is the first step toward building more authentic and effective relationships. The following exercise offers a simple way to begin exploring these patterns.

A Win-Win Exercise
Communication Self-Assessment

Effective communication isn't just about what you say—it's about how you say it, where you say it, and whether you're truly listening. This exercise will help you become more aware of how you're showing up in conversations.

Part 1: Assess Your Listening Skills

Think about a recent important conversation. Ask yourself:

1. Were you fully present, or were you thinking about your response while the other person was speaking?
2. Did you ask follow-up questions to show genuine interest?
3. Were you listening to understand or listening to reply?

Part 2: Check Your Body Language

Consider how you physically show up in conversations:

1. Do you make appropriate eye contact?
2. What does your posture communicate? (Are you open and engaged, or closed off?)

3. Are you aware of your facial expressions and what they convey?
4. How do you position yourself in the room? (Behind a desk? Sitting beside someone? Standing?)

Part 3: Evaluate Your Delivery

Reflect on how you deliver your message:

1. What is your tone of voice? (Warm? Harsh? Rushed?)
2. What is the pace of your speech? (Do you speak too fast when nervous?)
3. Are you adapting your communication style to make the other person comfortable?
4. Have you considered the environment? (Is it private? Neutral? Appropriate for the conversation?)

Part 4: Show Empathy

The most powerful communication tool is empathy—genuinely trying to understand where the other person is coming from:

1. Are you showing interest in the other person's hopes, dreams, and challenges?
2. Can you put yourself in their shoes?
3. Do you follow up on important topics from previous conversations to show you were truly listening?

Remember, people are more likely to hear your message and accept feedback when you've built trust through understanding, which requires empathetic, attentive communication.

With the above exercise in mind, choose one upcoming conversation where the stakes matter. Before you walk into it, consciously consider the above elements of communication. How can you adjust your approach to ensure that your message lands the way you intend? Understanding your communication style is a way of bringing greater self-awareness to every interaction.

What Happens When Communication Gets Complicated?

> *"The most precious gift you can give someone is the gift of your time and attention."* –Attributed to Nicky Gumbel

There's an idea that communication is something of an art form, but I'd suggest that it's more of a science. People inherently embody certain personality styles that influence how they interact with the world and see their place in it. DISC is one way of understanding this concept and allows for a more targeted approach in terms of how we interact with others. Even without a formal DISC assessment, EI can help us recognize where others are coming from and approach them with curiosity and compassion rather than judgment and assumption.

Communication is a skill that will serve you well in every facet of life, whether you dream of becoming a Fortune 500 executive or simply want to enjoy meaningful relationships in your personal life. With that said, it isn't always easy. Learning to communicate effectively also requires learning how to have difficult conversations. Good communication skills become even more essential when addressing conflict and can ultimately determine whether that conflict is resolved satisfactorily—or not.

CHAPTER 6

Mastering Conflict Resolution

Effective conflict resolution is all about getting to the win-wins. One of the best examples I know of how tension can transform into positive outcomes for both sides is "The Great Orange Debate." This is an exercise I often use when teaching negotiation in my leadership trainings.

The exercise begins by setting up a scenario where two parties each need oranges for different purposes. The room is divided into two groups, one representing doctors and the other representing medical researchers. At the center of the debate is The Great Orange. This magical fruit can be used to cure a specific illness (important for the doctors) and also to develop cures for diseases (important for the researchers). Each group has to make a case for why *they* should get the orange. Initially, this appears as pure competition—does the orange go to the doctors, who could save lives now, or does it go to the medical researchers, who could save lives in the future?

What the groups don't realize—at first—is that neither one needs the whole orange to reach its goals. Through careful dialogue and questioning (helped by the person proctoring the activity), the real discovery emerges: The doctors only need the rind of the orange to cure their patients, while the medical researchers only need the juice to further their science. This introduces participants to the powerful concept that most conflicts aren't truly zero-sum and that both parties can actually get what they need. However, if the groups don't take the time to listen to one another and communicate effectively, they'll never figure that out.

The Great Orange Debate exemplifies a situation where two sides seem to be completely at odds but can in fact reach a win-win solution if they engage with one another deliberately and with care. Of course, in the real world, things are usually more complicated. It's unlikely that a debate will have such a clear-cut conclusion as in this example. Still, the principle holds: Conflict resolution is all about communication, and if you are going to achieve win-win outcomes, you need to master difficult conversations.

Different Conflicts, Different Approaches—Always Honest

"Living with integrity means ... speaking your truth, even though it might create conflict or tension." –Attributed to Barbara De Angelis[14]

There is no one "right" way to approach every conflict. There are different approaches leaders (and anyone) can take, and the best one will depend on the exact circumstances—and the communication style of the individual opposite them. Regardless of the approach taken, the most important thing when approaching conflict is honesty. If honesty is lacking, that is going to create mistrust, and a lack of trust is going to make it very difficult to achieve a win-win outcome.

---

14   [Barbara De Angelis?], "Living with integrity means ...," Goodreads, accessed September 19, 2025, https://www.goodreads.com/quotes/7791-living-with-integrity-means-not-settling-for-less-than-what.

When people don't trust one another, they tend to become even more rigid in their stances as they attempt to protect any potential vulnerability. In contrast, when people are honest with themselves and others, it becomes easier to build trust and develop a type of synergy with others.

Depending on the people involved, their communication styles, and the context, the solution can be approached in a few different ways. Adept leaders will adapt according to the situation when deciding which of the following paths to pursue, determining how assertive they want to be in pursuing their own goals versus how cooperative they want to be with regard to the concerns of others:

1. **Avoid:** When you take the avoidant approach, there is a deliberate decision to take *no* action—one or both parties opts to stay out of the conflict completely. This results in an inevitable lose-lose scenario. Now, sometimes this moment will be temporary, and by giving both sides a chance to cool off, it can actually be a good thing. This pause can also allow for additional information gathering. However, the avoidant style can't be a long-term solution because it will allow issues to continue mounting.

2. **Compete:** When you embrace the competing style, you may be willing to satisfy your own interests at the expense of the other party's. In this scenario, one party attempts to get their own goals met without any regard for the other party's goals. This results in a win-lose outcome. It's a very assertive approach, but it's not very cooperative. With that said, this approach can be useful in encouraging team competition when creating new product ideas and it is used in sports.

3. **Accommodate:** The accommodating style is very cooperative but not very assertive. You actually prioritize the other party's goals and act unselfishly, giving up on your own goals. It's a very generous approach, but it means you aren't getting what you need. By satisfying others, you maintain cooperation. While this can feel like a loss, it can be effective in other ways—for example, by building credibility or creating leverage that you can use at a later date to address an issue that's more important to you than the current one.

4. **Compromise:** When you adopt the compromising approach, you're seeking a middle ground where both parties make some concessions to reach a workable solution. This results in a partial win-partial lose outcome for both sides. It's moderately assertive and moderately cooperative. This approach can be particularly useful when goals are important but not worth the potential disruption of more assertive methods, when you're dealing with mutually exclusive goals that need a temporary settlement, or when you're under time pressure and need a quick resolution.

5. **Collaborate:** When you embrace the collaborative style, you're working together to find a solution that fully satisfies both parties' interests and goals. This results in a true win-win outcome where everyone gets what they need. It's both highly assertive and highly cooperative, requiring commitment from all parties to work through differences creatively. While this approach takes more time and effort, it's the most effective for building long-term relationships and finding innovative solutions that address everyone's underlying interests rather than just their surface positions.

As mentioned, it's not only the context but also the communication style that can influence which of these approaches is appropriate. Knowing and appreciating the other person's communication style is helpful in resolving conflict. Knowing your own tendencies in a conflict can also help you approach difficult conversations with greater self-awareness.

A Win-Win Exercise
Assessing Your Conflict Style

Understanding your natural conflict resolution tendencies can help you become more intentional about when and how you engage in difficult conversations. This exercise will help you identify your default conflict style and consider how to adapt when different approaches might be more effective and so will get to the ultimate win-win collaboration.

Part 1: Assess Your Default Style

Read through each scenario below and choose the response that most closely matches your instinctive reaction:

Scenario 1: Your colleague consistently takes credit for ideas you've contributed in team meetings:

A. You avoid bringing it up because you don't want to create workplace drama.

B. You directly confront your colleague and demand they stop taking credit for your work.

C. You have a discussion with your colleague and let them take the credit.

D. You suggest a team process where everyone's contributions are documented.

E. You work with your colleague to find a solution that ensures fair recognition for everyone.

Scenario 2: You and your partner disagree about a major financial decision:

A. You postpone the discussion because it always leads to arguments.

B. You present your case firmly and expect your partner to see your logic.

C. You go along with your partner's preference after having a conversation about it.

D. You propose finding a middle-ground solution that partially satisfies both of you.

E. You schedule dedicated time to understand both perspectives and explore creative options to make the optimal decision.

Scenario 3: Your team is split on which direction to take for an important project:

A. You stay neutral and let the others hash it out.

B. You push hard for the option you believe is best, with no regard for the other parties.

C. You support whatever the others want.

D. You suggest combining elements from both approaches.

E. You facilitate a discussion to explore how both options might address underlying concerns and work to take the project in the right direction.

Part 2: Examine Your Patterns

Count your responses to identify your primary conflict resolution style. If you chose mostly *A*'s, you lean toward avoidance, meaning you often withdraw from conflict situations. If you selected mostly *B*'s, you lean toward competition, typically pursuing your own goals assertively. If your answers were primarily *C*'s, you lean toward accommodation, often prioritizing others' needs over your own. Mostly *D* responses indicate a compromise style, where you naturally seek middle-ground solutions. Finally, if you chose mostly *E*'s, you demonstrate a collaborative approach, working toward win-win outcomes that satisfy everyone involved.

Part 3: Expand Your Tool Kit

Consider situations in which your default style has served you well and identify scenarios where experimenting with other approaches might be beneficial. Remember, effective leaders can adapt their conflict resolution style based on the situation, relationships involved, and desired outcomes.

Remember, this is a simplified assessment for self-reflection. For deeper insights into your conflict resolution patterns, consider taking a comprehensive assessment.

Whatever style of conflict resolution you lean toward or pursue, you also want to assess the situation carefully before setting the stage. The resolution style that is appropriate for one situation may not be appropriate for another—for example, an approach that works well at home, with family, may not work well at work, with employees. The context matters when determining how to best approach a scenario. With that said, as a general rule, you don't want to go in tense and confrontational, but instead with an open mind and calm demeanor. A framework for difficult conversations can be helpful toward this end.

A Seven-Part Framework for Difficult Conversations

"When we avoid difficult conversations, we trade short-term discomfort for long-term dysfunction." –Attributed to Peter Bromberg

Anytime you find yourself stuck in conflict, there are crucial conversations keeping you there—conversations you're either not holding or not holding well. The following framework provides a systematic way to navigate those high-stakes discussions in which emotions run strong and opinions vary.

1. CREATE NEUTRAL GROUND

Make sure you're entering the dialogue open-mindedly and willing to hear the other person, not simply intent on defending your own goals. Begin conversations with something like "Let's talk about something that's important to both of us," rather than jumping into accusations or demands. Focus on what you really want from the conversation, and refuse to make anything an either/or choice. I often find that it's a good idea to let the other party speak first—it's a show of goodwill, demonstrating the fact that you really *do* want to hear the other person's point of view. Their point of view may end up bringing better solutions than you alone could have ever imagined.

2. EMBRACE THE POWER OF QUESTIONS OVER STATEMENTS

Questions can be used by both parties to promote engagement and reduce defensiveness while also giving both sides clarity. When you make a statement, it can feel like an attack, and the defenses go up—whereas when you ask a question, the defenses come down. The type of question you ask will depend on your DISC style and the style of the person you're communicating with, and adapting question styles to different DISC communication preferences can make your approach even more effective. Usually, "how" questions are calming—"How do you feel about this?" or "How do you see that?"—but there are some styles that may want to get to the point more directly. For example, a high-*D* person might respond better to direct "what" questions that get to the point quickly, while a high-*S* person might appreciate gentler "how" questions that allow them time to process their thoughts.

3. LOOK FOR COMMON GROUND

When asking questions, the key is to listen to understand, not just to respond. You want to understand where the other person's coming from. They probably do have at least one good point—and that is where you can start to build on common ground. Sometimes, you discover that you're actually saying the same things, just using different words to say them—so it sounds like you're disagreeing when really you're saying the same thing. I always use the image of a piece of toast to demonstrate this: One person wants to cut it into rectangles, and the other wants to cut it into triangles, but at the end, you still have two halves of bread. Is it really worth arguing about how the bread is cut?

4. APPRECIATE THE UNKNOWNS

Remember that in any conflict, there are always factors beneath the surface that you cannot see. The other person may be dealing with pressures, challenges, or pains that are completely invisible to you. Maybe they're facing a health crisis, financial stress, family troubles, or personal losses that you know nothing about. Imagine that person in a body of dark water: You can only see what's above the surface, and they may look completely fine there. But you can't know what's happening beneath the surface. Approaching conflicts with the awareness that there's always more to the story than meets the eye can transform how you respond.

5. MAKE MAINTAINING PSYCHOLOGICAL SAFETY A PRIORITY

Separate facts from the stories you're telling yourself about others' motives. Ask yourself, "Why would a reasonable, rational, and decent person do this?" rather than assuming negative intent. When you do speak up, focus on observable facts and your own experience rather than making accusations or having an emotional reaction. Establish a mutual purpose so that both parties feel safe to express their views honestly. When people feel psychologically safe, they're more likely to share their real thoughts rather than withdrawing or becoming defensive. Watch for when people shut down (silence) or become verbally aggressive (violence). These are signals that you need to step back to restore calm before continuing.

6. RECOGNIZE THE POWER OF THE PAUSE

Sometimes the best thing you can do is recognize when emotions are too high and suggest revisiting the conversation when both parties have had time to cool down and reflect. This prevents you from saying things you might regret and allows for more productive dialogue later. There's real power in simply stopping and saying, "You know what? Let's take a break. Let's stop for today and resume this tomorrow."

Maybe you need to get some rest, or maybe you need time to consider both sides of the conversation. The key is to respond, not react. Emotions don't last very long, but if you react to the person or situation in the moment, things are probably going to explode. When you start reacting, everybody starts reacting. But if you pause and let that emotion calm down, then you can respond from a place of logic rather than one of pure feeling—focusing on what has actually happened, not just how you feel about it.

The pause can also help you stay true to yourself. Many of us are people pleasers who want to keep everyone happy and maintain peace. But sometimes when you keep saying yes and being agreeable to avoid conflict, you're being inauthentic to yourself. There's power in saying no. Not only does it bring out your authenticity and what you believe, but it might actually be better for everyone else if you're being honest instead of trying to make everybody happy.

7. CREATE A PLAN FOR ACCOUNTABILITY

Once you've reached a point where you understand each other and have made progress toward an agreement—whether it's how you'll move forward or how to resolve the issue—it's important to hold each other accountable to what you've discussed. I always like to follow up in writing, which creates clarity and prevents misunderstandings later. Whether it's an email in a professional setting or a text message in a personal situation, the follow-up should capture the key elements of your agreement. Establish clear deadlines and check-in points. This framework ensures that good intentions translate into actual results and that both parties remain committed to the solution you've worked together to create, and it makes future solutions easier to accomplish.

One leader who has mastered the power of the pause is Lieutenant Colonel Joseph Loar, whose military career required him to adapt his communication style across vastly different cultural contexts. I coached him on civilian leadership, conflict resolution, communication strategies, and DISC, emphasizing in particular the importance of communicating across differences and recognizing the power of the pause.

MASTERING CROSS-CULTURAL COMMUNICATION

Lieutenant Colonel Joseph Loar, Retired,
Former Battalion Commander, 1-327 IN, 101st Airborne Division

Growing up as one of twelve kids, I developed my own approach to leadership at a young age: If someone else was willing to take charge, I was happy to stay in the shadows—until chaos threatened to take over—that's when I'd jump in to restore order. The natural inclination to maintain order shaped much of my twenty-year military career, from deploying to Iraq's Al Anbar Province to commanding paratroopers in the 82nd Airborne and, later, leading NATO operations supporting Ukraine. A military career teaches you that true leadership isn't about yourself—it's about the people you're leading. I learned that lesson the hard way when we had our first casualties in Iraq, and it influenced how I approached my interactions with my people from that point forward.

Working with Karen helped me understand the critical difference between management and leadership communication styles. In the military, we often say, "Don't bring me problems. Bring me solutions," but I learned to flip that script entirely and started telling my team, "Bring me your problems." This shift, along with my open-door policy, opened up the lines of communication in a really great way.

I have always enjoyed people of different cultures and different backgrounds—and the travel demanded by my military career gave me plenty of opportunities to do so—but DISC gave me a framework for understanding why people communicate the way they do, regardless of their cultural background. This framework became especially critical when I was assigned to lead one of the most culturally diverse teams of my career: a NATO assignment in Poland, coordinating aid for Ukraine.

When I arrived, I was overseeing a team of some thirty different nationalities who barely collaborated. They worked unilaterally with each other and seldomly coordinated as a group, specifically the Americans—which was especially challenging because the Americans managed most of the movement of supplies to Ukraine. While the NATO allies socialized in small groups with each other, the American leadership did not participate. There was a lack of trust rooted in unequal treatment in meetings and an unwillingness to engage in relationships to earn that trust. As a result, unified collaboration was practically non-existent, and a task that could have been done in two days—moving supplies from donor countries to Ukraine—often took two weeks. I wanted to change that and build one cohesive team starting with trust, as well as shared ownership of the project. I personally attended every social gathering and created new traditions like our "3k beer run." Through those interactions, we went from being thirty different "tribes" to being one tribe with a unified purpose. As a result of the improved collaboration, that job that used to take two weeks could be completed in two to three days.

"Sticking a pin in it" was a technique from Karen's class that struck me as particularly powerful in this cross-cultural context. In counter-insurgency warfare, we say "slow is smooth, smooth is fast." Another colloquialism in the Army is "combat patience," meaning slow it down, take a minute to let the confusion play out, and then make a decision based on good information, and act with speed and audacity. Karen gave me a more cross-cultural model that could appeal in a similar way—one of the most valuable being the power of the pause.

In American culture especially, we want to get it done now—we're driven by mantras like "time is money." But I learned that just because

> it feels urgent doesn't mean it is. Sometimes the best communication strategy is to put a pin in it and come back to it later. This approach has been extremely useful not just in command situations, but in life in general, because it prevents reactive communication and allows for more thoughtful responses. When things get chaotic, that thoughtful approach is crucial to restoring order—just like I did as a kid.

Lieutenant Colonel Loar has had to have many difficult conversations in his time as a military leader. His experience demonstrates how essential communication principles can transform even the most challenging collaborative situations—skills that prove invaluable whether you're leading a multinational team or navigating difficult conversations in a professional context.

Good Communication as the Basis for Meaningful Relationships

> *"Trust takes years to build, seconds to break, and forever to repair."*
> —Attributed to Dhar Mann

Conflict resolution is a skill that improves with practice and self-awareness. It also requires the courage to be honest about your own role in any misunderstandings. Sometimes, you have to take ownership of your part in the dynamic. The reality is that in any conflict, there's usually something you could have done differently. Perhaps you misunderstood their perspective, didn't listen carefully enough, got the timing wrong, or delivered your message with a too-harsh tone of voice. When you acknowledge your contribution to the situation and apologize genuinely for your part, it helps lower the other person's defenses and opens the door for productive dialogue. Sometimes, you have to let something sit, allowing the pause, to give others the time and space to understand and find clarity.

Good communication, especially in conflict, is one of the most effective tools you have for building trust and collaboration—the cornerstone of any meaningful relationship, personal or professional. It takes time to master these communication skills, just as it takes time to build trust. However, putting in the time to get it right is well worth it, because these communication principles not only help you navigate challenges but also form the cornerstone of meaningful relationships, personal and professional alike.

CHAPTER 7

Building Meaningful Relationships

People often talk about networking as being a key to professional success. I prefer to think of it as building meaningful relationships. This isn't a question of semantics. The reality is that when you focus on genuine connections that generate mutual value—instead of on transactional exchanges—you create stronger, more sustainable relationships. And those are the relationships that tend to have the greater impact.

I have moved around quite a bit in my career, and wherever I go, I always make a point of getting involved in the community, be it a local, state, regional, national, or even remote community. One way I do this is by joining the local chamber of commerce and getting involved with nonprofit organizations. Time and again, my participation in chamber activities has proven to be an amazing way to get to know my new community and the people in it while also contributing to that community in a meaningful way.

Through that community engagement, doors have opened to me that I could never have anticipated. My chamber involvement led to connections with educational institutions, city and county government officials, and local industry leaders. This exposure led me to a state leadership program, which then led to a regional leadership program, then a national leadership program—all of which had significant community service components. Thanks to the many service initiatives I participate in, I was nominated as a goodwill ambassador for the chamber. As a goodwill ambassador, I would attend ribbon cuttings for new businesses, support different local functions, and serve as a welcoming presence for entrepreneurs and business owners. It was all about greeting, welcoming, honoring, and supporting local businesses and the broader community.

My time as a goodwill ambassador for the chamber was incredibly rewarding, opening up new experiences and connections. However, it wasn't until a couple years later that I fully appreciated how this network of authentic relationships I had built could benefit not only me but the people around me.

It started with a chamber of commerce "speed networking" event. The format was straightforward: You had ninety seconds with each of fifteen different businesses to tell them about your business and hear about theirs. I sat down with a man who was the marketing director for a local advertising company that specialized in custom promotional items—stationery, pens, business cards, T-shirts, and so on. I was there representing the MBA program of the university where I was teaching at the time. On the surface, we had nothing to offer each other—he didn't need an MBA, and I didn't need promotional materials. But we had a really great conversation that went beyond the transactional nature of the event. And the following year, after building a relationship following that initial connection and recognizing his genuine commitment to the community, I nominated that man as a goodwill ambassador. Not only was he selected, but he went on to win Goodwill Ambassador of the Year—the same award I had won twice.

But the story doesn't end there …

A couple years later, still in academia, I was serving as an advisor to a sorority on campus. The young women at the sorority were active in a number of charitable initiatives. Our national philanthropic cause was breast cancer awareness. Someone suggested that it would be a good idea to have T-shirts for our "Think Pink" campaign. That's when I remembered my connection from the chamber—the marketing director for the local advertising company that specialized in custom promotional items. Guess who I asked to make our T-shirts? Not only did he provide the shirts at a reasonable cost, his company donated 10 percent of its sales that year to support breast cancer awareness.

But the story doesn't end there …

Breast cancer awareness is a cause that's long been dear to me. In college, I was the philanthropy chair for my sorority, organizing events to help raise awareness for breast cancer. From my chamber connections, I connected with the marketing director of a local hospital that was doing a breast cancer awareness campaign. I reached out to the director, and she agreed that the hospital would do a joint campaign with the sorority's "Think Pink" campaign, adding credibility and reach.

But the story doesn't end there …

I was very involved with athletics. I suggested that the sorority partner with that local hospital, which was the university athletics game sponsor, to create a joint "Think Pink" campaign handing out pink ribbons and self-examination cards prior to the game. Long story short: We ended up having a joint commercial alongside the local hospital on the big screen at a local university football game! One of my chamber of commerce connections worked in video and volunteered to produce the commercial. It featured a breast cancer survivor who was also an alumnus of the sorority and had been treated at the local hospital. All these threads came together in a fortuitous way.

The campaign was a huge success, raising significant awareness for breast cancer while creating an unforgettable experience for everyone involved. It also taught the young women in the sorority skills such as speaking, building relationships, and communication and instilled a newfound confidence in many of them.

When you get involved in things and step outside your comfort zone to help other people, you discover opportunities that you wouldn't have found otherwise. The relationships I had built over the years—with the marketing director, the people at the hospital, the university athletics department, and the young women at the sorority—came together, connecting everyone in a unified purpose and allowing for a real impact.

This particular story is concluded—for now. Who knows. Maybe in three, five, or ten years, there will be a new chapter because of the connections that were made through that initiative, and another opportunity to say, "But the story doesn't end there ..."

Community Engagement as Leadership (and Personal) Development

"I just give from my heart. I never know what I'm going to do or why I'm gonna do it. I just see a need and if I can fill it, then I will."
—Dolly Parton[15]

I think the story above demonstrates what I mean when I say that I like to differentiate between networking and relationship building. That anecdote shows the power of authentic relationship building, which goes beyond just exchanging business cards. You have to network to

---

15   Glenn Gamboa, "Dolly Parton's Donation Strategy Is to 'Just Give from My Heart,'" PBS, October 14, 2022, https://www.pbs.org/newshour/arts/dolly-partons-donation-strategy-is-to-just-give-from-my-heart.

meet people, then keep building the relationships. When you focus on adding value to others' lives, those connections create ripple effects that can benefit entire communities.

I honestly think this is one of the most valuable lessons any leader or future leader can learn. A lot of leaders talk about making an impact or making a difference. People who seek leadership positions often have a natural inclination to want to leave their mark, some kind of legacy. Well, what do you want that legacy to look like? If you want your leadership story to be more meaningful than corporate metrics that can be sketched out on a profit and loss statement, then your leadership must be more meaningful. Community engagement is one way to do that. Community can range from local to national or international engagement and service.

Community engagement is also an amazing leadership lesson. Getting outside of your comfort zone and getting involved helps you build your confidence, improve your communication skills, and gain a sense of perspective and humility—all things that make great leaders. It can also help you discover your authentic self and find your true purpose. When you try different experiences and meet different people through community service, you learn what resonates with you and what doesn't—what energizes you versus what drains you. You can meet some really amazing people you might not otherwise meet. That insight can also help you find your purpose in life.

Acts of service are also wonderful ways to keep learning, nurturing a growth mindset. There is always something to learn. There is always something to learn from the people you encounter through community engagement, regardless of their title, position, age, or background. Younger professionals may not feel like they have much to teach senior leadership, for example—but this is not true, in my experience. Younger generations are far more digitally literate, for example, and can help senior leaders navigate new technologies, such as AI.

When you approach community service with the mindset that everyone has something valuable to offer, you open yourself up to continuous learning and growth. This leads me to an important point about mentorship. Mentor–mentee relationships are often seen as the ultimate conduit for professional learning and growth. However, realistically, these relationships are not always easy to find.

I wouldn't say I've had one mentor in my career but many—people who have given me pearls of wisdom, offered advice, or simply listened when needed. I think some of these people would be surprised that I consider them mentors because these moments of interaction may have been fleeting and not strictly framed as a mentor–mentee relationship. However, that has not made them any less influential. This has led me to reframe the idea of what a mentor needs to look like. Instead of searching for one perfect mentor, I've learned to collect pearls of wisdom from many different people along the way.

One person who exemplifies this approach to mentorship and relationship building is Atin Suri. He is president of his chamber's young professionals network and a board director for the local chamber of commerce, in addition to being involved with various nonprofits. His dedication to community building exemplifies how authentic connections can benefit everyone involved.

BUILDING AUTHENTIC RELATIONSHIPS

Atin Suri, CEO, Suri Hospitality Group

I'm in the hospitality business, so relationship building means something very different for me than it might for other business owners. When I attend a chamber of commerce event or community gathering in

Arkansas—where my family runs a string of hotels—I see my peers getting direct business from their connections. But in my industry, it's a little bit different. The people I meet at these events live in the city—they don't need to book a hotel in the area. So, for me, these events are all about connecting with others to see how I can help them.

Karen is the person who helped me fully appreciate the value of this approach. She helped me recognize that I feel I am giving my best when I am genuinely connecting with other people. Through my work in the community, I've helped people get internships, jobs, resources—and being able to do that for others has been immensely rewarding. I also recently became an "onboarding aficionado" in our city, helping newcomers to the area with everything from questions such as "How do I pay my electricity bill?" to finding their place in the community.

In addition to helping me recognize the fulfillment that authentic relationship building brings me, Karen taught me several key principles that transformed how I approach others, from communicating with confidence and humility to making a good first impression. Even simple gestures matter—such as handing over your business card with two hands to show respect. However, I'd say the most valuable takeaway from her coaching, for me, was the power of building authentic relationships locally, regionally, nationally, and globally. It's not about immediate returns but about creating connections, developing as a leader, and making an impact on the community.

As I continue to grow our global family business in Kuwait, Dubai, London, Arkansas, and Texas, authentic relationship building remains a guiding principle in all I do. Beyond business, it's simply a good way to go through life, and I'm confident that this approach will continue to open doors—not just for me but for everyone I have the privilege to connect with.

Atin's journey perfectly illustrates how building meaningful relationships—rather than simply networking—creates opportunities that extend far beyond any single transaction. Our own connection has evolved over time, as he's gone from mentor to friend. I have met his family and had him to my home for Thanksgiving when his loved ones were out of the country. When he built a hotel from the ground up, I celebrated his success—and had the opportunity to bring my students there on a tour. And when he won Young Professional of the Year, I was at the banquet to recognize him.

Like anyone who meets him, I have been impressed by Atin's genuine desire to help others, something that allows him to connect with individuals from all walks of life, all over the world. The secret to Atin's success: authenticity.

The Art of Authentic Connection

"Trust is the glue of life. It's the most essential ingredient in effective communication." –Attributed to Stephen Covey

I often encourage the executive leaders I coach to attend business events and receptions, both industry association and nonprofit events, to practice building relationships. These events are perfect opportunities to work on making strong first impressions with actual business professionals who could potentially become mentors, employers, or valuable connections. The emerging leaders who take this seriously—who come prepared with business cards, dress appropriately, and approach conversations with genuine curiosity about others—consistently make the strongest connections and often walk away with real opportunities.

One group of emerging leaders I coached as part of a larger corporate development program turned one such networking event into a sort of competition. Their goal: to get the most business cards.

Was it a fun way to add some competitive spice to the activity? Sure. However, I had to remind them that the point of the exercise wasn't quantity but quality. It isn't about who gets the most business cards but about building meaningful relationships. That requires more time than a handshake, a hello, and an exchange of business cards. You need to actually get to know the person and have a real conversation with them to build a genuine relationship with them. One conversation of substance can go much farther than twenty superficial business card exchanges. To really build relationships, my students were encouraged to follow up on the connections they made.

The question is, how can you create an authentic connection, even in a short time frame? Here are some general pointers that can help.

FINE-TUNE YOUR FIRST IMPRESSION

We discussed first impressions in the previous chapter, but they warrant another mention here. When you're going into an event where you anticipate meeting a lot of people, it helps to get the basics down. Are you dressed for the occasion? Have you researched the occasion, cause, and any people of note you know you'll be meeting? If you're showing up to a business reception, for example, you might want to do your research and make sure you know who the leaders of the organization and the sponsors of the event are.

Some people think relationship-building skills just come naturally to extroverts, but anyone can learn the fundamentals of making a strong first impression. What happens in those first five seconds when you meet someone? You shake their hand properly and introduce yourself clearly, and they do the same. Your attire, eye contact, and whether you speak with authority and confidence all factor in immediately. Are you projecting nervous energy, or do you seem comfortable and self-assured? The more you practice these fundamentals, the better you get at them. It also helps to have some topics prepared for small talk so you're not caught off guard. Focus on the other person, and show genuine interest in their story. Practicing empathy builds stronger trust and relationships. The number one thing people like to talk about is themselves.

DON'T FORGET DISC

In the previous chapter, we unpacked the significance of DISC profiles and their varied communication styles. When you participate in events that expose you to a lot of people from different backgrounds—whether it's a community service initiative or a professional networking event, you will come across a lot of different communication styles. You then need to learn how to quickly notice someone else's communication style and adapt your own approach accordingly to have a good conversation.

This skill becomes invaluable in relationship building because it helps you connect with people more effectively from the very first interaction. For example, if you're talking to someone who seems more reserved and thoughtful, you might slow your pace and ask more open-ended questions. In contrast, if you're speaking with someone more direct and results oriented, you might get to the point more quickly. The ability to read these cues and adjust your communication style accordingly shows respect for how others prefer to interact—and serves as the cornerstone for a meaningful relationship.

PRACTICE INTENTIONAL INCLUSIVITY

Since I was a child, I wanted to treat everyone fairly—whether you're talking to the janitor or the CEO, you show up with respect. Imagine speaking to a new connection at a professional event—and witnessing them being rude to a waiter. Even if that person had been extremely professional and kind to you, you would probably think twice before pursuing any kind of professional relationship with them. After all, how someone treats people who can't do anything for them professionally reveals their true character. It should go without saying, but treat everyone with respect. You never know when a kind word or gesture may make someone's day.

In addition to respect, I personally try to make people feel special and valued. When I go to restaurants, I try to remember servers' names because it makes them feel valued, not just as people performing a service. This philosophy extends to how I approach leadership in any setting. When I'm doing speaking engagements, I move away from the podium whenever possible. If I have a portable microphone, or my voice is loud enough, I go into the middle of the room to actually interact with people. I don't want to be an authoritative figure talking *at* people; I want to talk *with* them. This creates a sense of connection instead of hierarchy—a step toward the kind of intentional inclusivity embodied by servant leaders.

BUILD TRUST THROUGH CONSISTENCY, IN WORDS AND ACTIONS

Meaningful relationships can't be built on words alone. Action is also required. It starts as soon as you meet somebody. After that first meeting, sending a quick follow-up—even if it's only to say that it was nice to meet them—is an action that shows you value the connection and are genuinely interested in maintaining contact rather than just collecting business cards. I still like business cards, although many people use electronic card-sharing apps now. Physical business cards help you build the relationship; they encourage you to remember the person's name as you make eye contact and say their name aloud to associate the name with the face. You can write a couple of facts you learned about the person on the back of the card to assist with the follow-up. I am also still a fan of the handwritten notecards. Not many people write these anymore, but I've found they're something many really appreciate.

As relationships develop over time, show true empathy by listening carefully and trying to understand others' stories, perspectives, and emotions. Consistency in words and actions is critical. If you say you'll do something … do it. It's that simple. Follow-through is crucial and reinforces that you heard and remember what the other person told you. That's how trust is built. And if there's nothing you can do for a person in the moment, the occasional check-in can still be a way to maintain a bond and nurture trust. During the COVID-19 pandemic, for example, I checked in on many people in my network, near and far, simply to say, "How are you doing? I know this is a tough time for all of us. Is everything OK on your side?" Those small actions can be impactful.

BE A BRIDGE FOR OTHERS

One of the most amazing things about building meaningful relationships is the connections that *you* can then create for other people. The opening story of this chapter exemplifies that. Connecting others is a wonderful way to add value beyond your own immediate needs and to build a sort of collective strength in your community. When you become known as someone who makes valuable introductions, people naturally think of you when opportunities arise.

This is what happens when you go beyond transactional networking to authentic relationship building. The result is true win-win scenarios that benefit not only you but those around you—making the time and effort you invest in building meaningful relationships *very* worth it.

A Win-Win Exercise
Building Meaningful Relationships

Authentic relationships aren't transactional—and in some cases, they can be transformational. This exercise helps you develop relationship-building habits that create value for others while strengthening your professional network.

Part 1: Gratitude in Action

Think of three people who have given you pearls of wisdom or made an impactful contribution to your life. Write each of them a handwritten thank-you note. Be specific about how they influenced you, whether it was convincing you to take a class or offering a simple word of encouragement.

Part 2: Everyday Relationship Building

When interacting with service workers (grocery clerks, servers, baristas), make an effort to remember their names and offer genuine compliments. Comment on something unique about them, comment on their positive attitude, ask how long they have worked there, or acknowledge them as a person in some other way. You never know what someone is going through, and these small gestures can brighten their entire day. For introverts in particular, these micro interactions can help improve confidence in communication, thus proving useful in the big picture as well.

Part 3: Community Impact

Identify one organization where you can make an impactful contribution to your community—your local chamber of commerce, United Way, Humane World for Animals, the American Cancer Society, or another cause that aligns with your values. Focus on where you can genuinely help, not where you might gain connections.

On a less formal level, you can also focus on small acts of service that build authentic relationships and create value for others. For the next week, ask yourself every day, "What can I do today to help someone?"

Remember, authentic relationship building is about what you can give, not what you can get. When you focus on adding value to others' lives, meaningful relationships naturally follow.

This mindset shift—from "What can I get?" to "What can I give?"—transforms not only how you approach professional relationships but also how you show up in every area of your life. When you consistently look for ways to help others succeed, support their goals, and connect them with opportunities, you become the kind of person others naturally want to work with, learn from, and recommend to others.

Authentic Connection: A Gateway to Success in Work and Life at Large

"I define connection as the energy that exists between people when they feel seen, heard, and valued; when they can give and receive without judgment; and when they derive sustenance and strength from the relationship." —Brené Brown

Building meaningful relationships through authentic connection can benefit you in any facet of your life. As you fine-tune these skills and implement them in your daily practice, you may find that new opportunities arise—even when you aren't looking for or expecting them. This foundation of authentic connection can also prove useful when you reach points in life where you want to make a bold move, like I did when I left academia for the corporate world.

This phase of the book has been all about relationship building. Why pay so much attention to the topic? Because leadership is fundamentally about influence through relationships—and strong relationships create resilience during challenges while accelerating success during opportunities. Further, when you've invested in authentic connections, you have a network of people who will support you through difficult times and celebrate your victories.

Authentic relationships provide a strong foundation for turning an idea into reality. But it takes more than authentic relationships to achieve your vision. In the next phase of the book, we'll explore how authentic leadership builds upon this foundation of meaningful relationships to create the kind of bold action that turns dreams into realities.

Activation

Taking Bold Steps

CHAPTER 8

From Dreams to Action

In the introduction to this book, I wrote about one of the boldest moves I've made in my life, though there have been many: my decision to leave academia. As I said, it was unexpected at the time. I had always thought I might want to do my leadership consulting and executive coaching full-time—*someday*. I had imagined this career step as something for my future, fifteen or twenty years down the road. But when the fortuitous opportunity arose to step into the corporate world, it felt like the stars had aligned, so I took it.

The opportunity itself came about in the most serendipitous way. I had been appointed by our provost to serve on a dean search committee tasked with selecting an executive search firm to help find our next dean. It was routine academic work—we reviewed five different firms, conducted Zoom interviews with three of them, and ultimately, invited one firm to visit our campus for final presentations.

When the chosen search firm arrived on campus, I approached their managing director to introduce myself, mentioning that we'd spoken during the earlier Zoom call. What happened next changed everything. Just five minutes into our conversation, he looked me directly in the eye and declared, "I'm going to hire you!" Then he paused, catching what he'd said, and added, "When you're finished with higher education."

The statement was so unexpected, so direct, that I instinctively glanced down at my watch—and asked myself, "What time is it?"

That declaration created a fork in the road. It felt like I had to make a decision: Was I ready to leave higher education already? It was a big question and one I didn't take lightly. In academia, I had achieved something that requires many years of dedication and which not all professors accomplish—tenure. For those unfamiliar with the academic world, tenure is essentially job security for life. It's difficult to obtain, requiring years of rigorous evaluation. I had started my tenure clock over three times by making the decision to move to other universities. Beyond that golden ticket of job security, I had a six-figure salary and excellent benefits. Not only that; I had received multiple awards for excellence in teaching and service, obtained numerous academic journal publications and academic conference publications, held positions as a Faculty Athletics Representative (FAR) and as the Sun Belt Conference FAR chair for four years, and served on the NCAA FARA executive committee. These were all big things to walk away from. However, the implicit invitation to step beyond academia sparked an excitement in me that went beyond mere curiosity. Recognizing that, I knew I had to seriously consider accepting it.

First, I wanted to do my research. I spoke to multiple people who could give me their perspectives on this potential career transition. I met with a woman who had been in academia herself before becoming the CIO of three Fortune 500 companies and asked for her advice. Her response was immediate: "Be bold; go for it. You may never get this opportunity again." I also sought out someone who had worked with executive search firms as a CEO client, wanting to understand what it was like to work with search professionals from that angle, and spoke to someone who worked for a search firm themselves. Finally, I asked a person who'd known me longer than anybody: my mom.

Armed with information, I was able to make the move with confidence. Now, shifting course wasn't an overnight process. It required deliberate goal setting, careful research, and thoughtful planning. It started with the articulation of the goal itself. That same day, inspired by my meeting with that gentleman, I scribbled it on a piece of paper—*Leave academia*—along with a set deadline: July 2022. It was March when I wrote that goal down. Four months later, I'd achieved it.

A lot happened in that span of time. On the piece of paper where I scribbled down my goal, I also wrote down a list of things that I needed to do to make it happen. My action plan included

- updating my CV,

- getting new professional headshots,

- talking to other people who had shifted from academia to the corporate world,

- meeting with my financial advisor, to discuss what-if scenarios and financial cushion planning,

- updating my LinkedIn profile,

- lining up references, and

- buying a new business suit.

And that was just the tip of the iceberg. In the end, I got a job with that same executive search firm that had come to campus to help us find a dean—the very firm whose executive had looked me in the eye and declared his intention to hire me when I was ready to leave higher education.

My preparation made the transition possible. If you're thinking of a bold move of your own, having a framework to help you implement it can be helpful. It starts with one simple step: articulating your goals.

Goals: From Dreams to Reality and a Greater Purpose

> *"A dream written down with a date becomes a goal. A goal broken down into steps becomes a plan. A plan backed by action makes your dreams come true."* —Attributed to Greg Reid

The first step toward reaching a goal is articulating it. Now, ideally, you'll do it in a slightly more structured way than I did when I scribbled down *Leave academia* on a legal pad. You may have heard of SMART goals in the corporate context, the acronym standing for goals that are specific, measurable, achievable, relevant, and time-bound. These parameters can be applied to your life, whether you're in pursuit of a professional or a personal goal. Here is what they may look like, with some personal illustrations to help illustrate my points:

- **Specific:** Set a clear, concise goal. In my case, I knew I wanted to leave academia—but my long-term goal was larger than that. I didn't just want to shift to the corporate world; I wanted to help people in it through leadership development and coaching. *That* was my long-term goal. Make yours similarly specific. Instead of "I want a better career," articulate exactly where you want to end up and the steps along the way. Maybe you want to target a specific role, company, or career path. Or maybe you want to start your own business.

- **Measurable:** Ensure you can track your progress. I gave myself very specific steps I could check off, from updating my CV to getting new headshots. Think about what concrete evidence will show you're moving forward. Maybe it's the skills you develop or the applications you submit. The key is having tangible markers that let you see your progress rather than just hoping you're moving in the right direction.

- ✿ **Achievable:** Make sure your goal is something you can realistically accomplish. I've always been one to dream big and have faith, but my goals still need to be within reach. This is where it's important to know yourself. For example, I would love to be the lead singer of a band—but I cannot hold a tune! That is not a goal I'm going to write down on a piece of paper because it would only lead to disappointment. In some ways, I've achieved that goal in a different form: I don't stand on a stage and sing for audiences, but I do have a microphone in hand when I'm speaking to audiences on leadership topics. Ask yourself if your goals are achievable—and if not, if there is a variation on them that might be a better fit.

- ✿ **Relevant:** Does the goal align with your values and long-term vision? My career move to the corporate world aligned with my desire to become a leadership coach/consultant. Ask yourself, "Does this goal fit with who I am and where I want to go?" If you value work–life balance, pursuing a goal that requires eighty-hour weeks might not align with your authentic self. The goal should feel like a natural extension of your values and interests, not something you think you should want.

- ✿ **Timely:** Set a deadline and create milestones. I gave myself until July 2022—just four months from when I wrote down the goal. I personally like to think about goals in different time horizons: short-term (six months to a year), medium-term (one to three years), and what I call my "someday" goals—those bigger dreams that don't have a firm date yet but represent where I ultimately want to be. The key is having something in each category and making sure they all connect to move you forward on your chosen path.

As you check off the smaller goals on your list, you will find yourself gaining momentum and confidence, but you may also discover something deeper emerging. While goals are powerful tools for creating structure and accountability, they represent just the beginning of your journey toward authentic leadership. The process of achieving these concrete objectives often reveals patterns about what energizes you, what creates meaning in your work, and what kind of impact you want to have beyond personal achievement. This progression from individual goals to something larger—your life's purpose and how you can serve others—is where true leadership begins to take shape. We'll explore this transformation more thoroughly in the later chapters of this book, particularly as we move into the leadership phase of your development. For now, focus on building the foundational habits that create momentum, knowing that each goal accomplished is a stepping stone toward discovering and living out your deeper purpose.

As a leadership and development coach, I have seen people trip over all kinds of stumbling blocks on their way to achieving their goals. Implementing a structured, strategic approach through goals can be helpful in addressing challenges. Here are a few of the more common issues I've seen people struggle with—and how goals can help.

TAKE ACTION INSTEAD OF PROCRASTINATING

Some people have a tendency to procrastinate. There are a lot of reasons for this, and I'll discuss some of those in the next chapters, in which we get into topics such as the psychology of change resistance. For now, I want to highlight how having a structured action plan through goals can be helpful in conquering procrastination by breaking things down into smaller, bite-size chunks of action. A goal that seems too big can be daunting and inspire a sort of freeze state. Break it down into something smaller, and you may find it easier to take the first step and get started. And that first step is critical to getting to the end goal.

COMMIT TO FOLLOWING THROUGH INSTEAD OF AVOIDING ACCOUNTABILITY

Follow-through is absolutely critical to achieving your goals—and to your credibility as a leader (or even as a trusted human). When you don't follow through on something you've committed to, particularly if you've made that commitment to other people, you risk losing both your credibility and your integrity. However, this principle of accountability doesn't just apply to commitments you make to others—it's equally as important to the promises you make to yourself. When you set those goals and create your action steps, you're essentially making a contract with your future self. Following through on those personal commitments builds self-trust and momentum.

TRUST IN THE PROCESS INSTEAD OF GETTING IMPATIENT

Some people, on the other hand, are the opposite of procrastinators: They want to get there yesterday! They want it done now! And they will do the work to get it done … But they might get frustrated when they don't advance as quickly as they'd like. The reality is that big dreams usually take time. A structured approach lets you see how the small wins are still moving you toward your destination, even if you aren't there yet. You're going through all the different steps and stages you need to achieve whatever dream you're pursuing. This can help you gain patience, reframing what might feel like passive waiting into a sense of active preparation for when the time is right.

KNOW WHEN TO PIVOT INSTEAD OF PERSISTING

Sometimes, you have to know when to adjust your approach—it doesn't mean that you're not committed to the goal or that you're changing it entirely. The key is understanding the difference between pivoting and persisting. Say you've been planning to launch your own consulting business by the end of the year, but then you discover that a major client at your current job is facing a crisis and needs your expertise for a critical project that could run several months longer than expected. You have a choice: Stick rigidly to your original timeline and potentially burn bridges, or pivot your timeline to honor your current commitments while still moving toward your ultimate goal. The smart move might be to delay your launch by a few months, use the extra time to build your financial cushion, and leave your current role on excellent terms—setting yourself up for long-term success rather than short-term satisfaction.

MAINTAIN MOMENTUM THROUGH SMALL WINS INSTEAD OF GETTING DISCOURAGED

Small wins deserve recognition—and celebration doesn't have to be elaborate or expensive. When I finally made the decision to write this book after putting it off for six months, I marked the milestone by opening what I would call a nice bottle of wine and having a glass to toast my commitment to moving forward. That was my celebration to self for making the decision to take action. Maybe your celebration is going out to a nice dinner, buying yourself a small gift, or sharing the accomplishment with a friend. The point is to acknowledge your progress along the way. Small wins deserve recognition—and that recognition can keep you motivated.

The key to making this approach work is putting it into practice systematically. The following exercise is designed to help you move from abstract dreams to concrete action steps you can start implementing immediately.

A Win-Win Exercise
From Dreams to Action Plan

Turning aspirations into reality requires more than just wishful thinking. It demands specific, actionable planning. This exercise helps you convert your dreams into concrete steps you can take, starting today.

Part 1: Vision Mapping

Write down what you want to achieve one year, three years, and five years from now. Be as specific as possible. Instead of "I want to be successful," write "I want to be promoted to VP of marketing at a Fortune 500 company," or "I want to launch my own business and have at least ten steady clients."

Part 2: Goal Analysis

For each goal, ask yourself whether it is:

1. Specific: What exactly do you want to do? Where exactly will this happen?

2. **Measurable:** How will you track your progress? What are your milestones?

3. **Attainable:** Is this something you can actually achieve, given your current resources and skills?

4. **Realistic/relevant:** Does this contribute meaningfully to your business or life? What will you get out of accomplishing it?

5. **Time-bound:** When do you want to have this accomplished?

Part 3: First Step Toward Commitment

Choose your one-year goal, and work backward to figure out:

1. **What do you need to accomplish in the next three months to get started on this path?**

2. **What do you need to do this month to begin?**

3. **What are three specific actions you can take in the next two to three weeks?**

Examples might include updating your résumé, getting your references in order, consulting with your financial planner, researching industry requirements, or working with an executive coach. Then, identify the very first action you can take this week to move toward your goal. Write it down, put it on your calendar, and commit to completing it within seven days (or even today).

Remember, the goal isn't to have everything figured out perfectly—it's to get specific enough that you can take concrete action. You can always adjust your plan as you learn and grow.

As you work through your action steps, commit to acknowledging your progress along the way. For each milestone you complete—whether it's updating your résumé, having that important conversation, or taking your first concrete step—decide how you'll celebrate.

Maybe it's as simple as checking it off your list with a sense of satisfaction, treating yourself to your favorite coffee, or sharing the accomplishment with someone who supports your goals.

Acknowledging those small wins is also a way to help build up your mindset—by making sure you recognize what you've accomplished and giving you a chance to pause and be proud of yourself. I've experienced the difference that a powerful sense of self-belief can make in my own journey—and I've witnessed it in others' as well. One person who exemplifies this beautifully is Cori Keller, whose journey from dreams to action demonstrates what's possible when you combine structured planning with unwavering confidence.

MAKING BOLD MOVES

Cori Keller, Healthcare Administrator, Baptist Health, and former Miss Arkansas

When I was first deciding on a career path, I was laser focused on becoming a physical therapist. After I got my exercise science degree, I interviewed for a physical therapy program, eager to kick-start my career. Well, you can imagine my shock when the interviewer stopped halfway through and said, "Cori, I don't think physical therapy is for you. I think you're going to hate it." She went on to explain that she felt my communication skills were an asset that wouldn't be put to good use as a physical therapist—and suggested I explore other options.

That conversation changed everything. I think getting a degree and then not using it is pretty bold—especially in such a niche field. But after reflecting on the interviewer's feedback and considering my own interests, I decided to reject my acceptance to the physical therapy program and pivot to communications studies—something completely new to me.

That pivot led me to the world of pageantry, where I further polished my presentation and communication skills, with Karen's help. I ended up becoming Miss Arkansas, a role that had me traveling all over the state, speaking at civic organizations, schools, and philanthropic events. I was only twenty-five at the time, and that experience put me in rooms with community leaders and decision-makers whom I would not have met organically otherwise. That's where Karen's coaching became invaluable.

Working with Karen, I refined my communication skills, discovered the power of DISC profiles, and learned mental strategies for staying calm and confident in high-pressure situations. I remember telling Karen how nervous I got presenting in front of people, and how she helped me reframe the situation, telling me, "Instead of saying 'I'm nervous,' try saying 'I'm excited.'" That small shift in language made a difference—and it was just one of the many tricks she taught me that helped me gain the confidence I needed to keep making bold moves.

My father was having heart problems during my Miss Arkansas year and was being treated at Baptist Health. Knowing he was watching the pageant on TV from his hospital room—it's the most watched summer programming in Arkansas, with over forty thousand viewers—and having seen how kind the staff had been to him, I gave both him and the hospital a shout-out on the final night of the competition. The hospital subsequently reached out and asked if I'd speak at future fundraising events, which led to me getting my current job as a physician liaison there. Today, my work is all about communicating and building relationships.

Women, especially in the South, are not always taught to be bold. Karen showed me that you can be a strong woman and don't have

> to be meek. The bold move to leave physical therapy behind opened doors I never could have imagined—and taught me that sometimes, the best opportunities come from saying yes to the unexpected. I'm currently pursuing my doctorate in healthcare administration and participating in an administrative fellowship program to become a hospital administrator. Because I'm not done making bold moves yet.

Cori's story illustrates what becomes possible when you stop waiting for perfect conditions and start taking action toward your goals. Her willingness to pivot when opportunities arise demonstrates the power of staying open to unexpected paths, and her commitment to making bold moves that honor her authentic self is a true inspiration.

Believing in the Process—and in Yourself

> *"You shouldn't be afraid of failing. You should be afraid of missing out on everything that you dream of because you lack the courage to try."* —Mel Robbins

Structured goal setting gives you a process you can trust in. However, you also have to trust in yourself. In addition to believing in your own abilities, it's helpful to have some greater faith—a knowing that it will all work out the way it's supposed to. Now, *faith* is one of those sticky words that can be defined a lot of different ways depending on whom you're talking to. I am personally a religious person, and so I have faith in God when the road gets rocky. However, I also recognize that faith looks very different for different people. My mother taught me that if you have the faith of a mustard seed, you can move mountains.

Some people may have a different religious or spiritual faith from my own that they fall back on. For others, faith may look like trust in the natural order of the universe—or simply a deep belief in their own resilience and ability to navigate whatever comes their way. However you define it, I think some kind of bigger-picture faith can be helpful, giving us the boost we need to get over the stumbling blocks that life throws our way (and they are inevitable), even when we are tired. This faith becomes especially important when we're working toward long-term goals that require sustained effort over months or years. It's what keeps us going when progress feels slow and when doubt creeps in about whether we're on the right path.

Faith can also give you courage—and courage is particularly essential when you're making bold moves. Maybe you've seen the poster of a kitten looking into a pond and seeing its reflection mirrored back in the water, except the reflection is actually that of a lion. That is the mindset I wish for you. Because while having a plan for a bold move is useful, when it's time to actually act on that plan, fear often becomes our biggest obstacle. In the next chapter, we'll explore how to gain the courage to make bold moves—confident as a lion, and sweet as a kitten at times.

CHAPTER 9

The Courage to Make Bold Moves

Imagine a large tree—let's say an old oak. The branches stretch high into the sky, covered in lush leaves. Birds make their nests in the greenery, while squirrels harvest the acorns the old tree drops for their sustenance. Unseen, but supporting this tree and its entire ecosystem, is the root network, twisting and turning deep into the earth. These roots ground the tree, keeping it firmly in place, no matter what winds may blow. They anchor the tree, rendering it an immovable object—destined to grow and grow in the same place, forever.

Hold that picture in your head for a moment. Now: Release it. Because *you* are not a tree. Unlike that tree, you are not stuck in one place forever, either physically or metaphorically. You have the ability to make bold moves and uproot yourself, be it from a city, a job, a situation … Unlike that rooted tree, you have the power to change your circumstances when the conditions are right.

I want to be very clear with this analogy: I am not saying that you should necessarily uproot your life and make some bold move, such as quitting your job, just for the sake of making it. I'm simply saying that you have the option and the power to make those changes, those bold moves, whenever the conditions are right.

This doesn't mean you should ignore genuine responsibilities or abandon people who depend on you. Like the tree, you might have some birds or squirrels that depend on your ecosystem, who thrive off the leaves and acorns you provide—these could be anything from work responsibilities to family obligations. Life has a way of presenting us with circumstances that require us to stay rooted, at least temporarily. Maybe you've been dreaming of moving to New York City to pursue a new career opportunity, but your mother has had a stroke and needs care. Maybe you have a child with special needs, or a spouse battling cancer, or elderly parents who require your support. These are real, significant responsibilities that can't simply be wished away with positive thinking.

Here's what's crucial, however: Sometimes we make our responsibilities heavier than they have to be. Take the example of wanting to move to New York City but having an elderly loved one to care for. You don't want to leave that loved one in the lurch, because it's important that you are able to lay your head on the pillow at night and feel that you've done right by people, especially those you love. However, sometimes, we take on caregiving as our complete identity, assuming there's only one way to handle the situation. We don't explore other options or have the difficult conversations that might lead to creative solutions. Maybe there are care facilities that could provide better support than you can alone. Maybe there are family members who could share the load. Maybe there's a way to bring your loved one with you to New York City or to structure their care in a way that still allows you to pursue your dreams.

The point isn't to abandon your responsibilities—it's to make sure you're not rooting yourself in place when there might be other paths forward that honor both your obligations and your authentic goals. Finding those alternative paths, however, requires something that doesn't always come naturally: courage. And courage, like everything else we've discussed in this book, looks different for different people. Understanding your own relationship with risk and bold moves, including where your courage might falter, is essential for making authentic decisions that you can stand behind.

Gathering the Courage to Make Your Own Bold Move

> *"A bird sitting on a tree is never afraid of the branch breaking, because her trust is not on the branch but on its own wings. Always believe in yourself."* –Charlie Wardle

There's an old saying that the greater the risk is, the greater the reward will be. While I do think that is true, to some extent, I also think it's important to note that risk can look different to different people. Knowing yourself and how you recognize, interpret, and respond to risk is useful when you're gathering the courage needed for a bold move. One way to do that is through an understanding of your DISC communication style.

For example, someone with a high-D (dominance) style might see a bold career move as an exciting challenge and be ready to act quickly, while they should probably slow down and do more research before leaping. An S (steadiness) style may be more hesitant about disrupting their stable situation and need more time to process the decision. A C (conscientiousness) style is going to want to analyze every possible scenario before moving forward—sometimes to the point of paralysis by analysis. And an I (influence) style might be drawn to a bold move simply because it sounds fun and exciting, without fully considering the practical implications.

Remember, no one is purely one style—we're all variations of all four, with different degrees of intensity. Sometimes, an opportunity may be so compelling that your DISC style doesn't matter; if you've researched the opportunity thoroughly enough, you're going to feel confident regardless of your natural tendencies. But understanding your default patterns helps you recognize where you might need to push yourself (if you tend to overanalyze) or slow yourself down (if you tend to act impulsively).

Knowing your communication style can help you in assessing risk more effectively. If you have a natural tendency to take risks, your decision-making process may look very different from how it would if you're risk averse. You may need to collect more information, talk to more trusted advisors, or give yourself more time to think through the implications. Depending on your style, you may want to approach the decision differently and research it differently.

The key question isn't whether you should take risks—it's understanding what you're willing to risk and how you define reward. Do you want to stay average, or are you ready to be awesome? Any DISC style can make a risky decision or a bold move and have the courage to do it—they may just approach it differently and need different types of assistance to make the decision. When I say assistance, that could mean conducting thorough research, preparing emotionally for the transition, saving money financially for a cushion period, or getting advice from people who've made similar moves.

Although exact approaches to risk assessment and decision-making will vary for the individual, there are a few things that anybody would do well to consider as they gather the courage to make a bold move. I've broken these components down into three core categories: authenticity, timing, and preparedness.

AUTHENTICITY: IS THIS MOVE APPROPRIATE FOR YOU AND YOUR GOALS?

In the previous chapter, we talked about goals and how important it is that your goals are both realistic and relevant. For example, while I might have dreams of singing on a stage, I know I can't carry a tune, but I have shifted to speaking onstage instead. It's a lot easier to pursue a goal with confidence if you know that it's both relevant and realistic to you, making it a good idea to reaffirm those parameters before going ahead. This ensures you're moving in an authentic direction that's true to you.

Authenticity is a good barometer when calculating risk because it speaks to what's true to *you* specifically—not your colleague, friend, or next-door neighbor. With that said, other people in your circle can have strong insights into who you are as a person, so collecting their feedback as you weigh a potential bold move and the risks attached to it is not a bad idea. I mentioned that when I made my transition out of academia, I spoke to multiple people in the corporate world first, including a C-suite executive who had made the move herself.

The question of authenticity also goes much deeper, relating to the idea of integrity. You want to make sure you are pursuing authentic goals with your bold moves; at the same time, you want to remain authentic to who you are as a person—and since most people don't exist as a lone tree but rather as part of an ecosystem of loved ones, that does mean considering those around you. When calculating risk, there are probably other people you need to factor into that calculation. Drawing from the example in the introduction to this chapter, this person could be a loved one you care for.

There are also less heavy, professional examples we might consider. Say you own a small business and have been approached with an acquisition offer. That could mean a nice chunk of change for you—but what does it mean for your employees? They are part of that ecosystem, the squirrels and birds in the tree, and also deserve consideration when you're calculating the risk (and reward) at hand.

Considering the implications that a bold move has for other people isn't about getting permission for your decisions—it's about approaching them with integrity. When we get to the win-win principles later in this book, we'll discuss how the goal isn't for the ends to justify the means. Instead, it's about finding the best possible scenario for everyone involved. In the case of making bold moves, the key is ensuring that your bold move serves your authentic goals while honoring your genuine responsibilities to others.

However, it's important to distinguish between genuine responsibilities and obligations we've unnecessarily taken on ourselves. Sometimes we make our responsibilities heavier than they have to be by assuming there's only one way to handle a situation or by taking on accountability that rightfully belongs to others. For example, if you're staying in a job because your team "needs" you, are you truly indispensable, or are you avoiding the discomfort of transition and change? The key is ensuring that your sense of responsibility stems from authentic commitment rather than from guilt, fear, or the need to be needed.

TIMING: IS NOW THE RIGHT MOMENT TO MAKE THE MOVE?

It's not always the right time to make a bold move. Sometimes, it's best to put off the bold move and wait for better alignment. In other instances, an opportunity will arise that will nudge you into making the bold move sooner than anticipated—as was the case for me when I left academia. I've seen similar scenarios play out for other people. A client of mine applied to be a supervisor at least five times over the years. He didn't get the position for whatever reason—maybe the timing wasn't right, maybe the leadership structure wasn't ready for his particular strengths. Then, finally, ten years in, he got the role, and now he's thriving in it. The right timing, the right leadership team, and the right organizational moment all came together.

His story is a testament to the fact that there are a lot of factors that impact timing, and you won't be able to control all of them. The time isn't always going to be right for a bold move, and sometimes that will be due to you, and other times it will be due to external circumstances. Say you want to start a franchise restaurant, for example. That requires a pricey up-front investment. If you're trying to minimize debt and don't want to take out a huge loan, you'll have to wait while you save up the money needed. And once you do have the money saved, the market still might not be right—for example, if you had planned on buying a franchise restaurant and then the COVID-19 pandemic hit, you'd probably have held off. It's not that you will *never* attain the dream. You just aren't attaining it right now.

When moments occur that delay a dream, it can be easy to feel stuck. Remember, a delay is not a denial. This is a good opportunity to reframe your mindset. Instead of thinking, *I'm never going to get there*, think, *What can I do today to help me get closer?* Maybe you can't open that franchise restaurant right now, but you can take a business management course, visit other franchise locations to learn from their operations, or start saving more aggressively toward your goal.

Making a bold move can sometimes start with those small steps that get you outside of your comfort zone. That doesn't require a dramatic life change—it could mean taking smaller steps that keep you moving forward. Join a nonprofit and do volunteer work, learn a new skill, listen to a podcast that helps you develop a growth mindset, or take a pottery class. These activities not only help you grow personally, but they also introduce you to new people and perspectives that might benefit you in unexpected ways down the road.

While you're at it, take a moment to appreciate the pause—think of where you are and how far you've come, while remembering that you're still learning and growing. You don't have to have everything figured out to keep moving forward. The key is to trust that you're not a tree, destined to be in the same place forever.

It's also important to recognize that you will never be perfectly ready, and there will never be a perfect time. Don't use fear as an excuse. The key is learning to distinguish between wisdom-based hesitation and fear-based hesitation. Wisdom-based hesitation sounds like "I need to save more money before I can afford this transition"—it's grounded in a practical reality. Fear-based hesitation, on the other hand, focuses on hypothetical worst-case scenarios: "What if I fail?" Don't let fear masquerade as wisdom and become your excuse for staying stuck.

PREPAREDNESS: ARE YOU READY PRACTICALLY, PHYSICALLY, AND EMOTIONALLY?

Finally, there is the question of preparedness when gathering the courage to make a bold move—and preparedness has many facets, from practical to spiritual. I've previously discussed the preparatory steps I took when I was considering leaving academia, from updating my LinkedIn profile to talking to my financial advisor. This last point was important to me because my parents had both worked in banking and had always ingrained in me a strong sense of financial responsibility. As soon as I was old enough to open my own checking account, my mother taught me how to balance my checkbook. I tease her and say she made me balance it down to the halfpenny. It had to be balanced!

Depending on the type of bold move you're thinking of making, you are likely to want to take similar steps. If you're looking at a career transition, you might need to update your résumé, network with people in your target industry, or acquire new certifications or skills. If the move is something more personal—say, switching cities—preparation might look like researching neighborhoods, securing housing, or building connections in your new location before you arrive.

Just as important as these practical pointers is the physical and emotional readiness that making a bold move requires. This brings us back to the idea of the oxygen mask. Do you have the energy to make this bold move right now? If you're already hanging on by a thread, exhausted and on the brink of burnout, the added burdens that come with a bold move such as changing jobs or switching cities may be too much right now.

Emotionally, making a bold move can be incredibly challenging, with a lot of ups and downs. You need to be emotionally intelligent— and even if you consider yourself emotionally intelligent already, you're probably going to learn to become even more so. You're likely to feel emotions you've never experienced before—at least, not at this intensity. Bold moves can be lonely, especially if you're moving to a new place or advancing to a higher level of leadership. There's truth to the saying that "it's lonely at the top"—the higher you climb, the fewer people there are who understand your challenges, and the more careful you have to be about confidentiality and trust. It is important to have a mindset of growth and solitude, as opposed to thinking of the situation as lonely.

The key is making sure you're prepared on every level. This can help you approach your bold move with both courage and wisdom. This chapter's win-win exercise can help you strike the right balance.

A Win-Win Exercise
Approaching Bold Moves with Courage and Wisdom

Making bold moves requires honest self-evaluation and careful preparation. This exercise helps you assess whether you're ready to make a significant change and ensures you're approaching that decision with both courage and wisdom.

Part 1: Authenticity—Is This Move Appropriate for You and Your Goals?

Before making any bold move, ensure it aligns with your authentic self and long-term vision:

1. Review your goals and purpose: Does this move advance you toward your authentic objectives, or are you moving away from something out of frustration?

2. Consider the implications: How will this decision affect other important people in your life? How can you approach this as a win-win rather than leaving others behind?

3. Talk to your network: Who is someone who's made a similar bold move to what you're considering? Have you reached out to them for advice?

4. Apply the "three to five trusted advisors" method: Identify three to five people you respect who can give you honest feedback about your potential move from different perspectives.

Part 2: Timing—Is Now the Right Moment to Make the Move?

Taking the right move at the wrong time can lead to unnecessary struggles:

1. Assess external factors: Are there circumstances beyond your control that make this the right or wrong time?

2. Distinguish between fear and wisdom: Are you hesitating because you're afraid or because your instincts are telling you to wait for better alignment?

3. Consider preparation time: Do you need additional skills, certifications, or experience before making this move?

4. Evaluate competing priorities: What else is happening in your life that might require your attention and energy?

Part 3: Preparedness—Are You Ready, Practically, Physically, and Emotionally?

Bold moves require comprehensive readiness across multiple dimensions:

Financial Preparation

1. Have you consulted with a financial advisor about the implications of your move?

2. Do you have adequate emergency savings (typically three to six months of expenses)?

3. Have you planned for worst-case scenarios and identified your options? Can you live within your means during a transition period?

Practical Preparation

1. Do you have the necessary skills, certifications, and/or qualifications?

2. Have you done your research about what this change will actually entail?

3. Do you have a support system in place for your practical and emotional needs?

Emotional and Mental Preparation

1. Are you emotionally prepared and strong enough to handle the intensity of feelings that come with major change?

2. Do you have healthy coping mechanisms and support systems in place?

3. Have you considered the potential loneliness or isolation that might come with your move?

4. Are you emotionally intelligent enough to think of the time as solitude for your own personal growth?

5. Are you prepared to feel emotions you've never felt before?

Remember, this isn't about talking yourself out of bold action—it's about ensuring you're making calculated, thoughtful moves that set you up for long-term success. Sometimes, the boldest thing you can do is take the time to prepare properly.

If you've completed this assessment and feel confident in your answers, you may be ready to make that bold move. However, if you find yourself still hesitating, take a moment to examine the source of that hesitation—is it coming from a place of wisdom or a place of fear?

Courage Brings Change— Change Brings Opportunity

"Great things never come from comfort zones." —Attributed to Jim Rohn

There's an important distinction between fear-based hesitation and wisdom-based hesitation. Fear-based hesitation often sounds like "What if I fail?" or "What if people think I'm crazy?" or "What if I'm not good enough?" These concerns focus on hypothetical worst-case scenarios and other people's opinions rather than on practical realities.

Wisdom-based hesitation, on the other hand, might sound like, "I need to save more money before I can afford this transition," or "My elderly parent needs my support right now," or "I should complete this certification first to be properly qualified." Wisdom-based hesitation is grounded in practical considerations and genuine responsibilities. Learning to distinguish between the two can help you move forward with confidence when the time is truly right rather than letting unfounded fears keep you stuck.

This chapter and the previous one have focused on equipping you with the tools needed to make decisions from a place of wisdom rather than a place of fear. Even with this careful preparation and consideration, once you *do* decide to make the bold move, you may still run into hurdles—and the biggest one will probably be your own mind. The next chapter looks at how to build a change-ready mindset that will allow you to persevere through the process of making a bold move and see it through.

CHAPTER 10

Embracing Change as Opportunity

When encountering a storm, many animals will seek shelter. Bison are unique in that they will often head into a snowstorm rather than drifting away from it with the wind. It's thought that bison do this because they instinctively know that walking into the storm will get them through it quicker.[16] There are photos of massive herds of bison, plowing their way through the snow, heads bowed as they walk methodically into the wind.

Sometimes, when you make a bold move, you may feel caught up in your own storm: The wind is blowing, the snow is swirling around you, and each step feels heavier than the last. While it can be tempting to scurry off in search of immediate shelter, doing so can often prolong the change process and, with it, your discomfort.

Instead, I encourage you to emulate the attitude of the bison and continue into the storm, head down and continuing forward, one step at a time. Of course, there are exceptions—moments when you should indeed pivot and seek proverbial shelter rather than persisting, which

---

16   "The Bison Advantage," National Bison Association, accessed June 20, 2025, https://nationalbison.org/the-bison-advantage.

we'll discuss. However, for the most part, this intentional, methodical, consistent approach to change is usually the most effective.

Even knowing this, executing a bold move and making a big change can be a nonlinear process where you are tempted to step sideways or backward rather than continuing on your path. In some cases, you may simply not know which direction to go in, and that indecision can result in stagnation. Therefore, indecision is a decision.

The difference between people who successfully navigate major changes and those who get stuck isn't necessarily courage or resources—it's mindset. Developing a change-ready mindset means learning to see uncertainty not as a threat but as a space full of possibility. It means reframing setbacks as course corrections rather than failures and viewing the discomfort of change as evidence that you're growing rather than a signal to retreat.

This chapter will help you cultivate this mindset so that when the storms of change inevitably come, you'll be ready to move through them like a bison: steady, focused, and confident that the storm will be over sooner.

Adopting a Change-Ready Mindset

"The secret of change is to focus all of your energy, not on fighting the old, but on building the new." —Attributed to Socrates

It's no secret that people are often resistant to change. There is an entire sector of psychology devoted to the topic of change resistance, which can occur for many reasons and take many forms. In the previous chapter, I explained how a person may perceive risk, depending on their DISC profile. Similarly, an understanding of your DISC strengths and weaknesses can help you understand how you approach change and what hang-ups you may face when trying to make a change.

For some people, change resistance is indeed a question of fear. They worry about the outcome of the actual change itself—or, perhaps better said, they question the outcome, which is technically unknown. After all, we can plan and prepare, but we can't guarantee results.

Others may not fear the change itself but the discomfort of the change process. They feel comfortable in the status quo and don't want to put forth the energy required to learn something new or adapt to different circumstances.

And others may fear the conflict that change sometimes incites. That starts with the internal conflict, the question of, "Am I really going to do this?" But it also extends externally. Depending on the situation, change often means difficult conversations with family members, colleagues, or stakeholders who may resist or question the person's decisions.

Those feelings of fear, worry, uncertainty, or anxiety can manifest in different ways:

- ✿ **Inaction:** Simply refusing to take any steps toward change, even when the current situation is unsatisfactory. Start with the smallest possible step—it will get you moving.

- ✿ **Indecision:** Getting stuck at the metaphorical fork in the road, paralyzed by what-if scenarios and unable to commit to a direction. Try switching your mindset to focusing on what could go right instead of what could go wrong.

- ✿ **Procrastination:** Continuously delaying the change with excuses about timing, resources, or readiness. Create a to-do list that breaks down steps into manageable tasks you can check off one by one.

- ✿ **Avoidance:** Steering clear of conversations, situations, or decisions that might force movement toward change. Consider other approaches or conflict resolution styles.

✿ **Analysis paralysis:** Over-researching and over-planning, to the point where the preparation becomes a substitute for action. Remember, 60 percent of something is better than 100 percent of nothing.

Diverse as they are, these feelings all keep us from moving ahead. Like a deer caught in headlights, paralyzed by oncoming traffic, indecision becomes a decision in itself—a decision to stay put in a potentially harmful or unsatisfying situation. When you avoid making a choice, you're actually choosing to let circumstances or other people's opinions decide for you.

Yes, something probably will go wrong—that's part of any change process. How do you break that cycle of doing nothing? Instead of getting caught in the swirl of what else could go wrong, get excited about what could go right. If you focus on the positive possibilities while having contingency plans for the challenges, you'll approach change from a position of strength rather than fear.

In the first phase of the book, we discussed methods you can use to develop a positive mindset and recognize your own self-worth, including repeating mantras, learning new skills, practicing creative pursuits, and journaling. This is the time to come back to those practices—they are your fountains of strength and continuity.

What hidden gifts might a transition reveal? This win-win exercise can help you unlock them—and, with those promising possibilities, unlock the change-ready mindset.

A Win-Win Exercise
Adopting a Change-Ready Mindset

This exercise helps you identify mindset patterns that either support or sabotage your ability to navigate transitions successfully. Think deeply about these questions and write down your responses.

Part 1: When Change Worked in Your Favor

Think of three times in your life when change went well for you—moments when a transition, opportunity, or shift led to positive outcomes. For each situation, consider:

1. What was your mindset during that time? Were you optimistic, curious, prepared, confident, or something else?
2. How did you approach the unknown aspects of the change?
3. Did you view your situation as a glass half full, half empty, or refillable?
4. What actions did you take that contributed to the positive outcome?
5. How did you handle any fears or doubts that arose?

Part 2: Learning from Difficult Changes

Think of one time when change didn't go as you hoped or something unexpected in life happened. Consider:

1. What was your mindset during that period?
2. How could you have perceived the situation differently?
3. What would you do differently now, knowing what you know about yourself?
4. In hindsight, did any good come from that difficult change, even if it wasn't apparent at the time?

Part 3: Preparing Your Mindset for Future Change

Consider a change you're contemplating in your personal or professional life right now:

1. What would be the first three steps you'd take to approach this change thoughtfully?
2. How can you cultivate a "refillable glass" mindset about this potential transition?
3. What patterns from your successful changes can you apply to this new situation?
4. How do you overcome fear?

Remember, the goal isn't to eliminate all uncertainty about change—it's to recognize that your mindset is the most powerful tool you have for navigating whatever comes your way.

Developing that change-ready mindset is the foundation to moving forward. You can then prepare to lead the charge, whether that means leading yourself as an individual or leading others as well.

Moving Through the Storm: Leading Yourself and Others

> *"Never assume that you are stuck with the way things are. Life changes every single moment, and so can you."* —Attributed to Ralph Marston

Even with a change-ready mindset, it's not always easy to keep moving ahead. Having a self-created change management system of some kind can help you stay the course. For me personally, I use my private calendar as my own mini change management system. I have a year's worth of calendar pages on my iPad. At the bottom of each calendar, I write the word "someday," with an arrow pointing to the next month. Every day, I try to mark off at least one thing I've done to move toward my goal, whatever that might be. Maybe it's listening to a podcast on entrepreneurship, thinking of a new leadership lesson, joining a seminar on improving speaking skills, meeting with a potential client to build a relationship, or joining a new industry association. The key is taking one to three small steps every day, or even every week, that keep me moving forward.

I love that calendar because I feel like I'm accomplishing something tangible, even when progress feels slow. It helps me balance being future oriented with living in the present, because while I'm working toward "someday," I'm also celebrating what I accomplished today.

Of course, some types of change require a more comprehensive change management system—for example, an organization transition. I once worked with a young CEO who had stepped into a new leadership position at a family-owned business. He was the outsider coming into this legacy company, and he had some really smart ideas on how to bring this former mom-and-pop shop into the modern age, such as updating technologies and implementing new performance metrics. However, he wasn't sure how receptive the company's board of directors, which still included the original owners, would be to this level of change. It was up to him to find that balance and ensure the company's core values and mission were maintained, staying true to the owners' vision, while the company's operational processes were modernized to allow for greater revenue, less waste, and increased profits. In the end, he was able to find a fitting approach that allowed him to strike that delicate balance—but it required careful consideration of both his own and others' priorities.

These two examples raise a critical distinction about change: Sometimes, you are only leading yourself through the change involved in a bold move, and that can present plenty of challenges on its own. However, at other times, you may be responsible for leading others through a change. You are the head of the herd, expecting others to follow. That status presents unique challenges of its own.

When you're the leader, you can't falter. Especially when it comes to a moment of organizational change, you have to execute decisions with clarity, changing what needs to be changed (say, as with the example above, operational procedures) while maintaining what needs to be maintained (say, the company's core values). It's important not to lose track of whether you're staying true to your personal core values and the organization's core values as you navigate the change.

When leading in times of uncertainty—such as during an organizational change—you have to be especially steadfast. Furthermore, you have to maintain calm. If other people see the leader panic, it creates a ripple effect of anxiety throughout the organization. Your ability to stay calm becomes a stabilizing force for everyone else. This intentional display of certainty also requires some level of discretion. You have to make decisions without being able to share all the information, whether they're confidential HR matters or strategic moves that require careful timing to communicate effectively.

Finally, and perhaps most importantly, a leader must also be prepared to have difficult conversations. Change inevitably creates resistance, and you're likely to get pushback from people who are comfortable with the status quo or fearful of the unknown. This is where understanding communication styles—such as the DISC profiles we've discussed—becomes invaluable. Being prepared for these different types of resistance and knowing how to address each communication style can help you navigate difficult conversations more effectively and bring people along with you through the change process.

As you can see, managing change gets to be a much bigger job if you're also managing other people while doing it. That's why the final phase of this book, starting with the next chapter, focuses on leadership.

The Transformation

"Not all storms come to disrupt your life. Some come to clear your path." —Attributed to Paulo Coelho

Whether you are weathering the storms of change alone or with a herd of followers to guide, a few principles remain the same. First, focus on moving forward rather than seeking immediate comfort. Second, stay true to your core values while remaining flexible about your methods and processes. Change what needs to change while preserving what truly matters. Finally, approach discomfort with curiosity rather than fear, recognizing that growth often feels uncomfortable but leads to transformation.

There is one last thought I want to leave you with as this chapter concludes—and that's the fact that these bold moves and changes we have been discussing can ultimately all add up to a larger transformation, one driven not by titles, awards, or external validation, but by passion, momentum, and meaning. This is where your true authentic self can shine.

Leadership

Creating Win-Win Impacts

CHAPTER 11

Leading with Authenticity

S ome people call me The Cat Whisperer. Yes, part of the reason for this is because I do love cats, having always owned at least one ever since my father gave me my first kitten at age two. However, the real reason for the nickname is my ability to herd (proverbial) cats. During a Harvard Executive Education class on authentic leadership, we were asked to write down our purpose. After reflecting deeply on what drives me, I wrote, *Herding cats to create excellence.* That was almost nine years ago, but it still rings true today. Throughout my career and personal life, I've consistently found myself taking chaotic, scattered situations and bringing them to a more stable, unified state. My DISC profile reflects this, categorizing me as a "conductor," and knowing this about myself allows me to lead with authenticity.

Living and leading with authenticity starts with knowing yourself. What are your strengths? What are your weaknesses? What drives you? What sparks your curiosity and motivates you? Only once you are able to recognize those essential truths about yourself can you create a space where others can comfortably do the same. It's like being the conductor of an orchestra: The maestro needs to know the song, recognizing the rhythms and the transitions, in order to lead the musicians accordingly.

I had this thought recently when attending a concert dedicated to the works of Whitney Houston. The songs were interspersed with clips of the famous singer herself, and when she spoke about her song "Greatest Love of All," she revealed that it's not a romantic song but one about learning to love yourself. *That* is the greatest love of all.

Loving yourself starts with knowing yourself—and that is the key to authentic leadership. It isn't about having all the answers. It's about knowing yourself well enough to guide others with clarity. What are the transformative experiences in your life that have made you who you are? There is the story of your life, and there are the facts of your life, and understanding yourself requires examining the facts, not just the narrative you create for yourself. That's how you're able to use your past to grow and go forward.

That past can be difficult. We have all experienced things that challenge us, from a personal illness to a death in the family, the loss of a job, or a big breakup. Whatever form they may take, these pivotal moments shape you, for better or worse, depending on how you let them. They form your real self. And there's no better place to lead from than your real self.

Authenticity Rooted in Empathy

> *"Honesty is not always easy, but it is the path to self-discovery and self-improvement. It requires courage, vulnerability, and a commitment to personal growth."* —Original source unknown

Throughout high school, I was a member of the color guard—performers who accompany marching bands, executing choreographed moves with flags. When I became the captain of the color guard, I knew I would have to start not only participating but also leading. That required motivating my team as well as training them on the technical side of things, fixing any mistakes.

One of the biggest mistakes that can happen in a color guard is someone dropping their flag. If someone dropped their flag during practice, I had to address it. In the past, I'd seen color guard captains ask a person to run laps or do push-ups if they dropped a flag. It might seem like a punitive measure today, but back then, it was a standard approach. I decided I wanted to lead differently, so instead of having them do push-ups or run laps alone, I'd join them.

I didn't realize it yet, but this was a nod to my "conductor" DISC style: wanting to bring people into unity. It was also a type of servant leadership. There is a saying that you shouldn't ask an employee to do something you wouldn't do yourself. By joining in with the push-ups, I was demonstrating that I was not only a leader but also a part of the team—through the good and the bad—and that I was not there to demean or dominate but to serve the interests of the team.

Servant leadership requires authenticity—in fact, authenticity is identified as one of the cornerstones of this style of leadership.[17] It enables the leader to show others that they can be themselves, while reinforcing other principles of servant leadership, such as interpersonal acceptance and stewardship.

In my view, authenticity must be rooted in empathy if it is going to be effective. Empathy means showing interest in others' hopes, dreams, and talents. By allowing you to put yourself in others' shoes to understand their emotions and perspectives, empathy builds stronger relationships, helps with communication, and fosters collaboration. It encourages you to really listen and take meaningful action on what is learned so the other person feels truly heard. People are more likely to take on feedback and listen to you if you build trust through understanding.

---

17   Dirk van Dierendonck, "6 Key Servant Leadership Attributes, " IEDP, September 26, 2011, https://www.iedp.com/articles/six-key-servant-leadership-attributes.

It's said that it takes years to build trust and only a moment to break it. This is why consistency in your values and actions is so important. When you compromise your principles, you risk destroying relationships that took years to build. I've learned that if you're going to make a mistake or change course, you should own it openly rather than trying to hide it. People can forgive honest errors and evolving perspectives, but they struggle to trust leaders who operate with hidden agendas or who abandon their stated values when it's convenient.

It basically comes down to what I call the "do right" rule. Are you doing the right thing for others, for the situation, and for yourself? Balancing all three can be difficult, and this is where authenticity comes into play—because ultimately, you need to do right in a way that upholds who you authentically are, maintaining your principles in a way that you can live with. If you look back in five years at a decision, will you be at peace with it? If you lead with authenticity and empathy, rooted in honesty, fairness, and kindness, the answer will likely be yes.

HONESTY

Knowing your real self is the basis for authenticity, but it's also the basis for acting with honesty and integrity—two essential leadership traits. If you make tough decisions as a leader, everyone may not like them. But if you make them and communicate them with honesty and integrity, people will at least respect you.

Honesty is the best policy, and it also requires some sense of self-awareness. Sometimes, when you're torn or trying to make a tough decision, whether it's personal or professional, you have to be really honest with yourself about your own wants, needs, and biases. That type of internal honesty is just as important as external-facing honesty, that is, being honest with other people.

FAIRNESS

Honesty and integrity go hand in hand with fairness, which is essential to building trust. When I was still in academia, I made it a point to treat my students fairly, whether it was how I graded their papers or whom I called on in class. I may have had students who didn't like my class or my teaching style, but I never had a student accuse me of being unfair, because I made a point of approaching them all equally.

KINDNESS

While we don't often speak about kindness when it comes to leadership, I do think it's essential. Authentic leaders understand that sometimes the person who attracts the most attention—whether it's the employee who's struggling the most or the team member who seems to be causing the most disruption—may actually be the one who needs the most support.

This instinct was shaped in me from a very early age. I remember when my dad took me to pick out a kitten, and I chose what you might call the runt of the litter: the smallest, sickliest-looking one.

When my dad asked why I'd picked that one, I told him, "Because that's the one that needs the love most."

That simple childhood moment taught me that sometimes, our greatest impact comes from investing in those who need us most, not those who are already thriving. Whether it's the struggling employee, the overlooked team member, or the person everyone else has written off, authentic leaders have the courage to extend kindness where it's needed most.

Now, this doesn't mean that you become a pushover. It's still important to be firm and set boundaries. For example, when it comes to identifying the person who needs the most support, remember that sometimes, that person is *you*. You may need to put your own oxygen mask on first before you can help others. Leading with honesty, fairness, and kindness doesn't mean neglecting your own well-being. It means recognizing that sustainable leadership requires you to maintain your own capacity to serve others effectively.

Setting Yourself and Others Up for Excellence

> *"Leadership is not about being in charge. Leadership is about taking care of those in your charge."* —Simon Sinek

When you're acting authentically from a place of honesty, fairness, and kindness, leading will get much easier—because you are connecting with people first before trying to command their respect. No matter how valid your message is, if people don't respect you, they aren't going to want to listen to it. Before people decide what they think of your message, they decide what they think of you. Being able to connect helps pave the path to a win-win: a situation where both you and those you lead can find harmony.

As a leader, you have a choice in how you show up. Do you lead with your credentials—your degrees, expertise, and accomplishments—or do you lead by connecting with people first? If you come in with warmth, you build trust. If you come in with competence, you build credibility. The key is finding the balance of both.

When you connect first, you don't have to *demand* respect. Instead, you command it naturally. People choose to follow you because they trust you, not because they have to. However, if you project competence or strength before establishing warmth, you run the risk of intimidating others rather than inspiring them.

It sort of just comes down to one thing: *Be nice.* I've seen the difference a little niceness can make, time and again. At one organization I worked with, I was on the review board to determine whether colleagues should be promoted. I found that others on the board focused almost exclusively on lack—what was missing from the person's CV that was holding them back. Well, if you solely communicate to a person all that they're doing wrong or lacking, that's not very motivating, is it?

So, I chose to highlight what they had already brought to the table. What were their success stories? Where did their strengths lie? What were they already doing well? Then, we could talk about what gaps they might address. It was a much more inspiring, encouraging way to get these people on the right path toward promotion. It was all about setting them up for success.

Being nice is a secret leadership superpower in my world. I truly believe it's the key to setting others up for success. People need to feel safe with you before they can truly hear your message. By creating a psychologically safe space informed by authenticity, you take the first step in setting yourself and others up for success—in short, you're taking a step toward a win-win.

With that said, being nice isn't about avoiding conflict or feedback. Being nice is simply a way of being; it's not about changing your attitudes or opinions or compromising your principles or your authenticity. Whatever you say or do, there is always going to be a critic. That's why leading with authenticity is so important: It ensures that you are staying true to you, even when faced with unfavorable feedback or even pushback.

An authentic self-assessment can help you identify the past challenges that have shaped you, as well as your current values, strengths, and weaknesses. This win-win exercise is a starting point for articulating those authentic parts of yourself.

A Win-Win Exercise
Authentic Self-Assessment

Authentic leadership begins with honest self-reflection. One of my natural gifts is "herding cats." What might yours be? Take time to explore these questions, which can help unlock your authenticity.

Part 1: Reflecting on Challenges That Shaped You

Reflect on a significant challenge in your life, such as a professional setback, personal loss, or moment when you had to take an unpopular stand. How did this experience change you? How did it help other people? What qualities did it reveal or develop in you? Often, such difficult experiences become the foundation of our most authentic strengths.

Part 2: Examining Competing Values in Moments of Conflict

Think of a time when you faced competing values or priorities—perhaps when doing the right thing professionally conflicted with you personally, or when being kind to a person also meant being firm with them. How did you navigate this tension? What did this situation reveal about your values? Sometimes, our most authentic moments emerge in moments of conflict.

Part 3: Identifying Your Natural Gifts

Consider a time when you felt most like yourself while leading others—perhaps when you were helping someone who needed support, bringing calm to a chaotic situation, or standing up for what you believed was right. What were you doing? How were you showing up? What felt effortless or natural about your approach?

Remember, the goal isn't to have it all figured out but to develop the self-awareness that allows you to lead from a place of authenticity, not from what you think others want from you.

Once you understand your authentic self, your natural gifts, your core values, and the experiences that have shaped you, you can begin to share that authenticity with others. The next step in authentic leadership is learning to recognize and validate the worth in those around you, creating an environment where everyone can contribute their unique strengths toward shared goals.

Moving Toward Your Greater Purpose

> *"Always remember that leadership is a privilege. When you're in a leadership role, your influence may affect the trajectories of people's entire careers (and often, their lives)."* –Attributed to Warren Bennis

As you step into authentic leadership and learn to set yourself *and* those around you up for success, you may find yourself confronting a critical question: What *is* success? It is ultimately about finding your purpose. Everybody defines success differently, so how do you define it for yourself? Is it titles, prestige, awards, and accolades? Is it simply happiness? Is it giving back to other people?

The answer matters because authentic leadership requires you to understand not only who you are but also where you're going and why. This question can also help you identify your larger purpose—the one that goes beyond accomplishing goals, feeling successful, and checking all the boxes.

Why does that larger purpose matter so much? Honestly, there will come moments in your leadership journey when you realize that all the external markers of success feel empty if they're not aligned with your authentic self—and part of that authentic self includes your true purpose. You might find yourself questioning whether the path you're on is truly yours or one that others expected you to take. These moments of reflection as you transition between who you are and who you are becoming are when authentic leadership is formed.

The next phase of your leadership journey involves learning to navigate these transitions with intention, understanding that authentic success isn't just about reaching a destination but about making sure you're taking the right step at the right moment. As with so many things in life, stepping into your purpose and yourself as an authentic leader is largely a matter of timing.

CHAPTER 12

Timing and Transitions

So much of life comes down to timing. Careers, romantic relationships, and even friendships can fly or flounder depending on timing—specifically, how they relate to the other things going on in your life at that precise moment. Our personal and professional development also often hinges on that elusive concept of timing. Getting the big promotion before you're equipped to handle the job can be just as disastrous as meeting "the one" before you're ready to settle down. Sometimes, we have to accept that the timing isn't quite right. A delay is not necessarily a denial but a time for preparation and growth. When the right moment comes, we often feel it and feel prepared.

That is how I felt when I left Virginia, where I had my first tenure-track professorship position. I really loved my time in Virginia, a state with beautiful nature and a great climate. I remember being so pleased by the lack of humidity, as it meant I had sleek, frizz-free hair for the entire time I lived there! I absolutely loved my job there. Still, there came a time when I knew I was done with that phase of my life and my time in Virginia. I was ready to move on to the next chapter.

Saying goodbye to Virginia meant saying goodbye to the house I'd bought there. It was a beautiful house, perched on a small mountain, which meant it had a really nice view. When you looked out the kitchen window, you could see these gently rolling hills, with the Blue Ridge Mountains in the distance. In the summer, it would be this sea of green as far as you could see. In the winter, those same hills would be white, covered in snow.

I remember walking through that house for the last time before I left. Everything had been packed up and moved out, the boxes in the truck, and what had once been my cozy home was now this big, echoing, empty space. It felt strange to see it that way, already waiting for the next person who would call it home, and even stranger to think that I didn't know what would come next. I was headed to Tennessee for a teaching position, and I wasn't really sure what my life there would look like. My social circles, my day-to-day routines, my job, and even where I would live—these things were all question marks.

That uncertainty scared me, but it was also an exciting moment. I knew in my heart of hearts that it was time to leave Virginia, as much as I'd loved my time there. I had moved about eight times in the previous ten years, and I had developed a sort of sixth sense for when it was time to move on—to shed the old and embrace the new. Transitioning to the next chapter of my life would require me to live in that liminal space for some time, existing literally between two places as I made my way to Tennessee. Even after I arrived, the metaphorical in-between would continue until my transition was complete.

I was not sure where I was headed, but I was confident that it was toward something that was more aligned with my authentic self and my true purpose. So, I put my faith in the process, said goodbye to that old house in Virginia, and went ahead, feeling at peace with my decision.

The Liminal Space: Occupying the In-Between While Trusting What Comes Next

> *"When it's time for something new, you will feel it. You will feel a desire to let go, to shed layers, to move, to recreate. You will know because there will be subtle shifts all around you. You will release the old because you're clearing the path for what's ahead. Trust this process."* —Attributed to Brianna Wiest

Time is one of your most precious resources, and time spent in transition, although sometimes uncomfortable, can be the most valuable and transformative. Transitional moments tend to be the most pivotal in our lives, often becoming moments of deep personal development. These moments can occur for any number of reasons, from losing a loved one to getting a new job, watching your adult children leave the nest, or entering retirement.

When you're transitioning to the next phase of your life, be it personally and/or professionally, there is often some ambiguity attached to that moment. This can result in all kinds of emotions, from unease to fear. Moments of transition can lead to uncertainty, not only about where we may be going but about who we may be becoming. There may also be discomfort, both emotional and physical (to return to the house metaphor: Consider that moment when you're mid-move, with half your boxes at one place and the other half at another, and you're just wondering where in this mess you've put your toothbrush).

Existing in the liminal space can be uncomfortable, but it can also be productive. When you get to this space, it's helpful to acknowledge that you can't control anything except your response to everything. And the truth is that even in these in-between moments, there are things we can control, and giving care and attention to these things can help us lean into the process of becoming and ensure it unfolds in a way that aligns with who we are and what we want out of life. Use this time to conserve energy, make space for growth, have faith, and appreciate the power of the pause.

CONSERVE YOUR ENERGY

A moment of transition is often an opportunity to recharge. In fact, because these periods of change can feel tumultuous, they often demand more rest than usual. Take time to rest and recover. You don't always have to be busy pushing ahead to the next thing. Step back and use this time to take care of yourself. Remember, sometimes you have to put your own oxygen mask on first before you can do anything else. Be patient with yourself, and don't get stressed if you don't see immediate results or if the transition is taking longer than you'd like. This is a rare chance to refill your proverbial gas tank.

There is a common misconception that to make the minutes count, we have to be active. In fact, a moment of intentional rest can be just as productive and worthy of your attention. Give yourself the chance to live life minute by minute, hour by hour, instead of day by day or week by week. High achievers in particular tend to be laser focused on where they're headed and want to always sprint in that direction. But even the most gifted athletes take time to rest. A sprinter isn't going to go all out the day before the hundred-meter dash. A long-distance runner isn't going to run a full marathon the day before a big race. Conserve your energy. Your future self will thank you for it.

MAKE SPACE FOR GROWTH

While you take time for rest in the liminal space, you can also make space for growth. Use this transitional period to explore things that interest you, and in the process, you will find yourself growing. You might attend a lecture in person, for example, or take a master class on a topic that you've always been curious about. This isn't about forcing yourself to be active but about exploring areas of interest that you are genuinely curious about and that you never had time to look into before. I once watched an entire master class video series on skin and skin care—it was incredibly intriguing! I was drawn to it because I had a skin cancer removed a few months prior. Those moments of discovery can be just as recharging as doing nothing. And as you're learning, you're often receiving exactly what you need to hear in that moment.

This kind of exploration helps further your authentic self-discovery while also pushing you beyond your usual comfort zone. Trying new things can be a great way to tackle negative emotions such as fear, anxiety, and uncertainty. It allows you to explore the unknown in a controlled way, be it through an online course, a tour, or a new social situation. The key is redirecting your energy toward possibility rather than paralysis. Instead of focusing on what could go wrong, train yourself to consider what could go right. This shift in perspective transforms uncertainty from something that immobilizes you into something that energizes you.

HAVE FAITH

It's important to trust your own intuition to guide you through the liminal space. A lot of people will listen to their mind over their heart, and while it's good to make decisions and act from a place of logic, that doesn't mean you should fully discount what your heart tells you. It's essentially about having faith. Again, faith can take many different forms, and I'm not dictating what it should look like for you. Some people may have a different religious or spiritual faith from my own. For others, faith may look like trust in the natural order of the universe, or simply a deep belief in their own resilience and ability to navigate whatever comes their way. Ultimately, I think it comes down to having faith in yourself—and in the process. Listen to your heart, but ensure that your heart is listening to the facts. This balance sharpens your intuition.

Trust that you will emerge from the liminal space headed in the direction that works for you. If you can balance the pull of your head and your heart, you'll gain greater clarity, but you have to give it time. Having faith helps you know that everything will fall into place at the right time, and that can bring great peace of mind. It will also help you avoid destructive behaviors, such as "keeping score"—always trying to assess whether you've given more than you've received or accomplished more than others around you.

APPRECIATE THE POWER OF THE PAUSE

In the chapter on conflict resolution, we discussed the power of the pause in difficult conversations. Similarly, there is great power in the pause in the liminal space. Take the time to let it develop. Don't rush it. You don't have to respond to everything immediately. Be calm and don't react immediately. Instead, pause before responding—and know what is worth the energy of a response and what isn't. You don't have to respond to everything.

This is a lesson I had to learn myself, as I'm the type of person who wants to jump into fix-it mode immediately. The problem is that when you try to rush things, you end up making decisions based on incomplete information or emotions rather than clarity. You might force solutions that don't truly fit, or worse, you might miss opportunities that would have become clear with a little more patience. It's OK to take a deep breath and slow down instead of going full steam ahead, which has been a lesson for me. It is harder for some people than others.

It is generally acknowledged that it's best to have a difficult conversation after any intense emotions (hurt, jealousy, fear, joy, happiness, etc.) have passed because if you're reacting from an emotional state, you're probably lacking clarity. Never reply when you are angry, make a promise when you are happy, or make a decision when you are sad. Similarly, when it comes to transitional moments, it's best to take action after you've gained clarity on the situation. With time, that clarity will come. The exercise that follows is designed to help you find that clarity by connecting with your authentic vision for the future.

A Win-Win Exercise
Visioning Your Next Chapter

This exercise helps you visualize your next chapter in life in a way that aligns with your authentic self and true purpose. When you combine clarity of vision with intentional action, you can bridge the gap between who you are now and who you want to be in the future, creating momentum in the act of becoming.

Part 1: Recognizing the Signs of Transition

Think of a time in your life when you had to trust yourself or your intuition about a major change. Maybe it was when you felt yourself detaching from a job, relationship, or living situation that no longer served you. How did you bring yourself through that transition? What role did timing play? What did you experience in that shift that made you realize you were on the right path?

Part 2: Trusting the Liminal Space

Reflect on that period of uncertainty between your old situation and your new one. What did you learn about yourself during that in-between time? How did you navigate the discomfort of not knowing what would come next? What growth can you see, looking back on that time now?

Part 3: Manifesting Your Vision

Now, turn your attention to your current transition or the next chapter you are contemplating. Instead of creating a traditional vision board, engage in detailed visualization. If you're considering a career change, what do you want your new office to look like? What city do you want to be in? If you're thinking about relocating, visualize your ideal home in specific detail—what view do you want from your kitchen window? What does your morning routine look like in this new space?

Remember, the goal isn't simply to do more but to do what matters most. Your next chapter should align with your authentic self and serve what truly matters to you.

After you've completed this visualization exercise, take a moment to notice how you feel. Is there a sense of clarity? Calm? Inner peace? That sense of serenity that comes from envisioning an aligned future is the same energy you'll need to create win-win outcomes going forward.

The Calm of Authentic Alignment: Setting the Stage for Win-Win Success

> *"If you don't make the time to work on creating the life you want, you're eventually going to be forced to spend a LOT of time dealing with a life you don't want."* –Kevin Ngo

The reality is that you never know how much time you have on this earth. You can always pull up your bank account and know how much money you have left. But there's no such option for time. With that in mind, it becomes all the more important to make the most of every moment, asking yourself, "Is this moving me in the direction I want to be moving in? Is it aligned with my authentic self? Does it support my larger purpose? Will it get me to where I want to be? And as I move in that direction, am I appreciating the process itself?"

Accepting the essential truth that time is scarce can actually bring great calm and clarity. When you stop fighting against the natural rhythms of transition and instead learn to work with them, you discover that timing isn't something that happens to you. Rather, it's something you can learn to navigate with intention. This allows you to take any anxiety you may have about the unknown and repackage it as excitement about possibility.

The sense of calm that comes with being aligned authentically with your true self and your purpose is what you will need to get to the win-win—or, better said, the win-*wins*, because the truth is that there isn't one huge win-win in life. It's a series of win-wins, situations where everyone grows and moves forward.

It's important to understand that win-wins aren't perfect. When you reach a win-win solution, you can't control how the other party reacts or whether they immediately recognize the value of the outcome. It may take time for them to realize what a great solution it is—or they may never fully agree with you. That's OK. A win-win doesn't mean everyone is thrilled or that there's complete harmony. Sometimes it means you agree to disagree and everyone moves forward anyway. You're being authentic, you're listening, you're being empathetic, and you're trying to do the right thing—but you can't be responsible for how others choose to perceive or respond to the outcome. What matters is that you've created a solution where everyone can move forward, even if imperfectly.

These win-win moments require all the skills we've explored: authentic self-knowledge, effective communication, conflict resolution abilities, and the wisdom to recognize when the timing is right to act. The final piece of the puzzle is learning to create these win-win outcomes consistently.

CHAPTER 13

Creating Your Win-Wins

One of the few pieces of jewelry I wear consistently is a pearl ring. It is something very meaningful to me in many ways. Depending on the culture, pearls carry all kinds of symbolic meanings, from confidence to purity and integrity. Some say that a pearl is a teardrop fallen from heaven. I treasure my pearl ring, and I got my mom a matching pearl for Mother's Day after my father had completed his cancer treatment—an acknowledgment of the perseverance both she and he had shown through that difficult and transformative time. In my mind, that is what pearls represent above all: transformation through difficulty. After all, that is how pearls are made.

Pearls come from oysters. They are created when an irritant, usually a grain of sand, enters the mollusk. The mollusk coats that irritant with layer after layer of nacre, a combination of calcium carbonate and conchiolin, the same material that makes up the oyster's shell. We commonly call nacre mother-of-pearl. Over time, these layers upon layers of nacre build up to create a pearl.

To me, it's a difficult yet beautiful origin story. The moments in our lives that are the most disruptive—the moments when the proverbial grit gets into our protective shell—are often the most transformative. And those are the times that can produce the most astounding result: a pearl.

Similarly, the journey to win-win outcomes can be difficult, but that difficulty is part of what makes the result so meaningful and impactful. Just as the oyster transforms an irritant into something precious, we can transform our challenges into opportunities for creating outcomes where everyone truly benefits.

Pearls are notoriously delicate and need to be treated with care. I remember when I got my ring, I was warned to always remove it when doing something manual, such as washing dishes or moving furniture. Knocking it on a hard surface could easily result in a scratch. Even wearing it while sleeping could cause damage because of the friction of it rubbing against the sheets.

While I've done my best to be careful of the ring, it's not quite as flawless as it was when I first got it. There are some slight scratches, and maybe it's lost some of its luster. But to me, it's just as valuable as ever. Those imperfections reflect the reality of life: It's not going to be perfect, but the imperfections don't diminish the value. They're part of the story. And when we are faced with the imperfections, the trials, and the tribulations, we carry on. We make the most of life despite the imperfections, seeking the win-win wherever we can.

And there is more than one win-win to be had. Life is a series of win-wins. Just because you've achieved one win-win—be it the promotion or the partner or some other achievement—doesn't mean that you're done. There are more win-wins to be had, and they can take different forms and result in different outcomes. The end result they share is that they leave you in that state of peace, calm, accomplishment, and alignment, giving you that feeling that you're in the right place, at the right time, doing the right thing.

That's not to say that everything is perfect when a win-win materializes. Like a pearl, a win-win itself is not perfect. It may be slightly uneven or scratched. It's not about perfection but excellence. And you want to enjoy and make the most out of that moment of excellence, because like pearls, win-wins require ongoing maintenance, nurturing, and care. Even when you reach an excellent place, you'll need to shift, adapt, and tend to what you've created.

At its core, a win-win isn't about reaching a destination where you'll finally be happy and peaceful. It's about finding peace and serenity in the journey itself—being happy and peaceful along the way, even as you work toward meaningful outcomes where everyone involved gets what they truly need.

My mother has always told me, "You're either going into a storm, in a storm, or getting out of a storm in life." Life is constantly shifting, and so are win-wins. Just as the bison doesn't wait for the storm to pass but moves through it, you have to keep adapting and adjusting.

Life as a String of Imperfect Pearls

"Good things come to those who believe, better things come to those who are patient, and the best things come to those who don't give up." —Original source unknown

Life isn't always easy. There are going to be plenty of moments when you've got a bit of grit in your shell, and it will be uncomfortable, and you'll just have to trust in the process and know that a pearl will be born of that discomfort. In short, when faced with grit, you've got to show grit—the kind of tenacity and perseverance we discussed in chapter 3. This will allow you to transform that irritant in your shell into something beautiful. The way you react to that bit of grit and persist will determine the luster of the pearl that emerges. After all, pearls come in all sizes, shapes, and colors, from black to milky white and pale pink. What kind of pearl will you create? What kind of pearl do you *want* to create?

This book has given you the tools you need to help shape that pearl to the best of your abilities. With each part, we've covered a topic that can help you get to the win-win and create your own pearl:

- **Foundation**—understanding and preparing yourself

- **Connection**—building effective relationships

- **Activation**—taking bold steps

- **Leadership**—creating win-win impacts

With this essential framework, you can create your own win-win, again and again. It will be a process that demands repetition and consistency, because a win-win is not a continual state. Like the tides of the ocean, win-wins ebb and flow, which is why you need to keep working at them. And just like a string of pearls coming together, one win-win can lead you to other situations where you'll need to create yet another win-win. Each successful outcome becomes part of a larger pattern in your life—a series of moments in which you've learned to navigate challenges and come out the other side with something beautifully imperfect.

Sometimes you'll have to work harder at it than other times. And when the win-win moments shift, you'll need to learn how to shift and adapt accordingly. That adaptability will make it much easier to deal with the proverbial grit in your oyster shell. Accept that you'll need to adjust. The oyster doesn't try to get rid of the grit—it turns it into something beautiful. You can do the same. It comes down to many of the things we've discussed: knowing yourself, recognizing your worth, being able to communicate effectively with others, controlling your reactions, continuing to grow, tackling difficult conversations, and—perhaps most importantly of all—enjoying the process.

Sometimes we get so fixated on where we're going and the prized pearl we envision at the end of the road that we miss the fun of the journey. That means missing out on some of the most essential parts of life: the development, the growth, the *becoming*. And it's a real shame to miss out on those integral moments. So, give the process just as much attention as the outcome—and be kind to yourself along the way and have some fun because that will make the sometimes-challenging journey much easier.

Taking care of yourself is essential if you're going to make it through the ups and downs of the win-wins. That means addressing the essentials: eating, sleeping, moving your body. However, it also means addressing the mental component. Are you taking time to check in with yourself? Give yourself kudos for what you've accomplished? Appreciate what you've done?

Have faith in yourself, and have faith in the process. Have faith in general, however that may look for you. Like an oyster, know that something beautiful is going to come from the grit in your shell. It might take longer than you'd like. And it might take all kinds of twists and turns to get there. But it will come. Faith.

When I was a little girl lining up my baby dolls as my "students" in my pretend classroom, I never could have foreseen that I would actually go on to become a college professor—and then an executive leadership coach, speaker, and author! I was just tapping into something I enjoyed doing: helping others grow. As it turns out, that is and always has been my core purpose—my "second mountain." I was living it as a child, even without recognizing it. It would be decades until I realized that purpose as an adult. It took years of studying, teaching high school mathematics, and getting a PhD to become a professor. And it wasn't until I'd spent years in academia that I made my bold move to leave and pursue executive coaching. But I got there.

Looking back, the moments that got me here—the string of imperfect pearls, of win-wins—all make sense. Sometimes, it's by looking back that we are able to more clearly see our path forward. The following win-win exercise is designed to help you do exactly that.

A Win-Win Exercise
Rediscovering Your Authentic Thread

The activities that brought you the most natural joy as a child often contain clues to your deepest purpose and most effective leadership approach. Take a moment to reflect on the following questions.

When you were younger, what were three things you were really good at?

Think beyond formal skills or school subjects. Maybe you were the kid who could make anyone laugh or the one who organized elaborate games that got everyone involved. Perhaps you were naturally good at listening when friends had problems, or you had a talent for noticing when someone felt left out.

What were three things that brought you tremendous joy?

What activities made you lose track of time? What did you do when no one was telling you what to do? Consider not just the activities themselves but the essence of what made them joyful. Was it the performance aspect, the teaching element, the creativity, helping the one who needed love the most, or the connection with others?

How do these childhood gifts show up in your adult life?
The child who loved putting on shows might naturally command attention in boardrooms or find fulfillment in public speaking. The kid who organized neighborhood games might excel at bringing diverse teams together. Someone who added theatrical flair to ordinary moments might be the leader who knows how to make work engaging and memorable.

Remember: The goal isn't to abandon your adult responsibilities and return to childhood but to recognize that your most authentic strengths were likely visible very early in your life.

Now that we've looked at the best parts of you, consider the future. Where do you want to grow to next? What will your pearl look like? And what do you need to do to create space for it?

A Pearl in Progress

"Strive not to be a success, but rather to be of value."
—Attributed to Albert Einstein

A pearl in an oyster presents a sort of mystery. You can't know what it's going to look like until you've shucked the oyster and gotten into the shell. Similarly, the win-win can be a bit of a question mark at times. It might not look like how you imagined. I never imagined getting a PhD until a well-intended professor suggested it to me. I never imagined leaving academia when I did until an interesting opportunity I hadn't anticipated appeared. And I hadn't planned a book until someone approached me with the option. These were all surprise pearls.

It's good and smart to articulate your dreams, strategize around them, and work toward them, crafting your win-wins along the way.

But the truth is that sometimes the most exciting win-wins are those that take us by surprise—the hidden pearls we couldn't have seen coming. When those moments arise, you often have to simply listen to what your heart is telling you. Again, it comes down to faith, be it faith in a higher power, faith in the process, or simply faith in yourself and all that you are capable of. I am a person who's very much driven by a combination of intuition and logic, so I know firsthand how challenging it can be to shut off the pragmatic arguments and follow your intuition.

The question is, when a pearl comes your way, will you be ready to receive it? This book has been created with the intention of helping you achieve that win-win state of mind: calm, peaceful, receptive, and ready. The goal is to find stability—a steady state that allows you to sustain yourself through the highs and lows. Remember, there are pros and cons to everything, give and take in any opportunity, and consequences to every decision you make. You just have to figure out what's right for you, even if someone else wouldn't define it as right. It comes back to how you look at yourself in the mirror. This is the essence of the win-win: It's not about perfection but about living with authenticity and an openness to the beautiful pearls life may present to you so that you're ready to receive them. One after the next.

Winds of Change

Just like you can't control the ocean tides or the weather, you can't control life. One day, the sun may be shining on a dazzling azure ocean. The next, the clouds roll in, and that same blue ocean looks dark and foreboding. Regardless, there are pearls to be found beneath the surface of the waves. Being able to navigate the waters with calm and serenity will ensure that you can find them.

When the storms come and the water is churning, remember: It's only temporary. Those difficult times still serve a purpose and, in some cases, can be some of the most fruitful. Sometimes, the tough times are best spent in rest and refuge, recharging your batteries. Other times, the tough times are those that prove the most pivotal, transforming you in ways you might not anticipate. As the skies clear, you'll be able to assess the aftermath, and, if you've worked on articulating your authentic self and pursued the bold moves that reflect that, the next steps will become clear.

Even as one storm passes, the next may be brewing, so make the most of the calm waters while you can. Be the conductor of your own life, and remember, the "greatest love of all" is always for yourself. Don't settle for less, because you deserve to be happy. Be tenacious. Follow your dreams. Make them happen. Accept that there will be moments of discomfort, perhaps even pain, and remember: That bit of grit entering the oyster shell will one day become a pearl. Trust in that fact—and trust in yourself, letting your courage and confidence exude.

Living and leading authentically is not without challenges. However, the hurdles it may pose are well worth the payout: living a life that truly aligns with your wants, needs, and vision. And when you do live your authentic self, that will draw people in and attract success. People are inspired by authenticity. By being *you*, you help others to do the same. It's a win-win for all. Be the example, the one who inspires others to dream and tap into their unused capacity.

Why wait? Time is precious, and you never know how much you have left. Don't waste it, and stay true to you. Because that's what matters most.

Finally, remember: You don't have to go it alone. I am here to help, whether you are seeking clarity in your journey, contemplating bold moves, trying to master conflict resolution, wanting to enhance your emotional intelligence, or simply hoping to unlock your true self. I look forward to helping you craft the pearls of your own win-wins.

Crucial Conversations: Tools for Talking When Stakes Are High, **by Kerry Patterson, Joseph Grenny, Ron McMillan, and Al Switzler.** The authors provide practical strategies for navigating high-stakes conversations where opinions differ, emotions run strong, and the outcomes matter deeply. The book teaches readers how to create dialogue instead of debate, stay in conversation when it feels easier to walk away, and speak honestly while maintaining respect.

Grit: The Power of Passion and Perseverance, **by Angela Duckworth.** Duckworth challenges the conventional wisdom that talent is the primary driver of success, arguing instead that grit—the combination of passion and persistence toward long-term goals—matters more than natural ability.

The Let Them Theory, **by Mel Robbins and Sawyer Robbins.** Mel Robbins offers a step-by-step guide on how to stop letting other people's opinions, drama, and judgment impact your life. All it takes is two simple words: Let them. It's a great reminder to put your own oxygen mask on first, among other things. Robbins also has a podcast and a YouTube channel.

Mindset: The New Psychology of Success, **by Carol S. Dweck.** Dweck introduces the distinction between two fundamental mindsets: the "fixed mindset," which assumes that abilities are static traits, and the "growth mindset," which embraces the belief that abilities can be developed through effort and learning from failure.

The Second Mountain: The Quest for a Moral Life, **by David Brooks.** Brooks explores the concept that life often has two major phases or "mountains" that people climb. The first mountain represents the conventional goals many people pursue early in life, such as career advancement, financial success, social status, and achievement. The second mountain is about finding deeper meaning and purpose beyond yourself.

True North: Discover Your Authentic Leadership, **by Bill George, with Peter Sims.** Written by a Harvard Business School professor, this book focuses on authentic leadership development through discovering your "true north"—your internal compass—based on your values, purpose, and understanding of yourself. It's all about pulling back the layers of the onion to learn your authentic self.

I would like to thank the talented team at Forbes Books for all the collaboration and help in making my vision come alive in this book. My deepest thanks to Lauren Garrett and Annie LaGreca for their guidance as my authority advisors, Lindsey Clark and Alison Killian for their thoughtful developmental editing, Heath Ellison for his careful editorial work in production, and Ruthie Wood for designing a cover that captures the heart of this book. I'm also grateful to Adam Witty, CEO, and Evan Schnittman, chief growth and publishing officer, for their leadership and vision in bringing this project to life. Thank you all for helping me share this message with the world.

DR. KAREN R. MCDANIEL is a leadership development consultant and executive coach and the founder of Empowering Executives. She holds a PhD in organizational behavior, human resource management, and strategic management, with additional studies in neuropsychology and marketing; and has spent over two decades in academia and corporate leadership development. Dr. McDaniel holds multiple certifications in leadership development, behavioral assessments, conflict resolution, and executive presence and specializes in helping leaders unlock their authentic potential through her tailored coaching, speaking engagements, and consulting services. Her work has spanned diverse industries, from hospitality to healthcare, and her clients range from corporate executives to aspiring entrepreneurs. Dr. McDaniel serves on multiple boards and remains actively involved in leadership initiatives. She continues to coach leaders and speak on authentic leadership nationwide.